LISTEN TO THE VINEDRESSER

Volume 2

*31 Declarations Of Who
You Are In The Vine*

BY
THERESA M. CROFT

Copyright © 2017 by Theresa M. Croft

Published by Kingdom Messenger Network, (KMN Publishing) 3148 Bomar Road Douglasville, Georgia 30135

No part of this publication may be reproduced, stored in a retrieval system, or transmitted in any form or by any means— for example, electronic, photocopy, recording— without the prior written permission of the publisher.

Scripture taken from the New King James Version®. Copyright © 1982 by Thomas Nelson. Used by permission. All rights reserved.

Scripture quotations marked (NLT) are taken from the Holy Bible, New Living Translation, copyright © 1996, 2004, 2007, 2013, 2015 by Tyndale House Foundation. Used by permission of Tyndale House Publishers, Inc., Carol Stream, Illinois 60188. All rights reserved.

Unless otherwise indicated, all Scripture quotations are taken from THE MESSAGE, copyright © 1993, 1994, 1995, 1996, 2000, 2001, 2002 by Eugene H. Peterson. Used by permission of NavPress. All rights reserved. Represented by Tyndale House Publishers, Inc.

Scripture quotations marked TPT are from The Passion Translation®. Copyright © 2017 by BroadStreet Publishing® Group, LLC. Used by permission.
All rights reserved.
ThePassionTranslation.com

To contact the author about speaking at your conference or church, please go to ikingsmedia.com/ contact.

I dedicate this book to Jesus Christ, My Father God
And the Holy Spirit.
Thank you for showing Your love by speaking to me.
I am thankful to be grafted into THE VINE with THE
VINEDRESSER taking care of me.

Table Of Contents

Introduction 1
Chapter 1 *Gold In the Fire* 2
Chapter 2 *Freedom In The Vine* 5
Chapter 3 *Beating Fear: Face-Time With Jesus* 9
Chapter 4 *Surviving Internal Pressures* 13
Chapter 5 *Loving Your Self (Soul)* 16
Chapter 6 *24 The Chariot Ride* 21
Chapter 7 *Inner Unity* 25
Chapter 8 *Turnaround In Your Health* 30
Chapter 9 *Zipping Fear* 35
Chapter 10 *God Says.. Turnaround* 40
Chapter 11 *Healing Shattered Hearts* 43
Chapter 12 *Pushing Back Anxiety* 46
Chapter 13 *My Lips Shall Praise You* 51
Chapter 14 *A True Valentine Love* 55
Chapter 15 *Steps To Turn Around* 59
Chapter 16 *Beating Barriers To Your Dreams* 63
Chapter 17 *Dealing With Pain And Trauma* 67
Chapter 18 *The Focus Word* 72
Chapter 19 *Winning Heart Battles* 76
Chapter 20 *The Gumby Stretch* 80
Chapter 21 *A Salute To The War Horses* 83
Chapter 22 *Eviction Notice To Fear* 87
Chapter 23 *Embrace The Yuck* 91
Chapter 24 *Open Door* 95
Chapter 25 *Held In The Grip Of Grace* 99

Chapter 26 *Communion: A Word From The Son* 102

Chapter 27 *Validation: The More Than Enough Anointing*..........107

Chapter 28 *Keys Of Favor* 111

Chapter 29 *Spark To Destiny Delay* 116

Chapter 30 *Keys And Open Doors*...121

Chapter 31 *Sweet Marriage In The Vine*..126

About..133

Introduction

This is your invitation from the Vinedresser, your Father God to take a 31 day journey with Him in this devotional. You are His child. He calls you much loved son, much loved daughter.

I believe as you draw near to Him, He will draw near to you and unveil the secrets of His Heart. He says in His Word that He will reveal deep and secret things. It's His delight to take you by the Hand for a walk through His Vineyard revealing tender thoughts and truths of His Heart.

That is what He has done for me the past five years as Holy Spirit speaks to my heart in the voice of the Vinedresser, the lover and caretaker of my heart.

This is Volume 2, by requests, of my thoughts amidst my journey as a revivalist.

I am His revivalist only because He has blown open the doors of my life disrupting the plan, pain, trauma and drama of the evil one. I candidly share my life with all the fears, tears, hopes, and dreams.

I have found that a key in walking in victory is being spirit lead, and speaking His promises with declarations. Then, resting in His presence to listen to what HE says makes all the difference for your destiny. So I hope you can speak out loud each declaration and then listen...LISTEN TO THE VINEDRESSER.

Chapter 1

Gold In the Fire

Read 1 Peter 1:3-8

What sustains you when you go through the fire of tragedy?

Your faith! And you get to witness gold in the fire.

Recently I spent a good amount of time in a whirlwind standing by a dear friend who tragically lost her daughter.

It's made me think of how precious life is. And how precious is faith and Kingdom family.

My friend, who is a mother in our church, has been a pillar of faith, peace, and hope through the trauma.

I had written a Vinedresser from a prophetic word (I had the notes of it) I gave to a prophetic husband of a friend a year ago!

I just feel this word is a good way to salute a mighty woman of God, my friend Pam, and those of you who display the majesty of God's love and grace even when life throws you a curveball.

First, this verse from the Passion Translation:

"Through our faith, the mighty power of God constantly guards us until our full salvation is ready to be revealed in the last time. May the thought of this cause you to jump for joy, even though lately you've had to put up with the grief of many trials.

"But these only reveal the sterling core of your faith, which is far more valuable than gold that perishes, for even gold is refined by fire. Your authentic faith will result in even more praise, glory, and honor when Jesus the Anointed One is revealed." 1 Peter 1:5-7 TPT

Declaration: I am His gold. I may be going through fire but I can trust God to guard me and bring out the gold in my faith.

Listen To The Vinedresser

"I see gold in that fire. You feel the heat but I see something even more precious than gold. Your faith in Me.

"Gold can always be found at the lowest, darkest places. Let Me turn a floodlight on for you. Allow My revelation to radiate in your heart for the life path ahead. Take My hand, beloved. Follow in the way of My overflowing kindness.

"Give me the shovel and lets dig in My Word, and not for you to dig a pit to camp. Ease your bruised heart in Me. The chipping away is only from those issues which keep you from intimacy, for which you are born for, with Me. I desire more gold of truth to come from you. Don't give up. Don't give in. Don't stop now.

"I allow tests in the process not to smother you but cover you in more of My tender care. Let My love nourish your heart. Embrace the process. Lean in to my faithfulness. Trust the timing of release with Me. I am overseeing every step and move. Just continue to hand the shovel over to Me.

"I have made you to speak for Me. My DNA is in the very cadence of your rich voice. You will are a strong tower for others. You carry the breaker anointing to see chains of addiction and any emotional bondage fall. Prosperity and My favor are yours which you freely pour out to others.

"Your intentionality for more of Me is bringing a great move of My Presence and anointing. Your heart is beating for restoration in marriages, families, and children. You life is a song of hope. I trust you dear one....For I see the glow of gold in the Fire.

"Don't give up. Don't give in. Don't strive...simply abide...in the Vine."

Love the Vinedresser

Chapter 2

Freedom In The Vine

Read Luke 4:16-19

What do you say when you feel you are in the jaws of the enemy? How do you make sense amidst madness of sin out of control, whether its your own or from someone else?

Can one find any true freedom in the Vine?

That was my question one morning before I headed out with my husband to our School's retreat a couple of years ago.

Freedom had been on my heart all week as one friend had texted me Tuesday afternoon about desiring complete freedom to walk away from abuse. From that text, the Lord lined up amazing words on freedom all week right into the weekend at the beach.

On Saturday while at Panama City Beach, we all circled around our Senior Leader Steve and Brent for baptism in the ocean. As they shared a prophetic short word over each person, each person proceeded to get dunked into the calm ocean waters. The emotion from each individual that came out of the water was priceless. From pure joy, with screams, to shaking tears, each person had their own personal encounter with God. Many had their journey in freedom in Christ solidified.

Freedom.

It is for you. Your life can radically shift and change as you open your heart and ask God to sweep into those areas of pain, drama, trauma, and shame. He is so gentle to pull out the arrows in your heart, cleanse the wounds, and bring sweet comfort.

God knows your heart too. It is often when you let go with your mind of how something will work out and trust with your heart that your desired breakthrough happens. Believe and trust from your heart....And worship while you wait!

So, with your freedom coming in to reality, a beautiful vessel of honor comes forth.

One thing is for sure, the Word brings so much living hope to guide you as you manage life's tests and have confidence in times of crisis.

As I was struggling last week with expressing thoughts on freedom, I went into the Vineyard in my heart and asked for Holy Spirit help.

This is what He gave me with a simple declaration.

Get a cup of coffee. Let's listen together what the Vinedresser said. But first, a declaration:

In the Vine Declaration: Jesus gives me freedom. I can live free from fear because His love conquers me.

Listen to the Vinedresser

"My child, I hear your cry for freedom. It is why My Son never lost sight amidst the litany of hostility in His faithful journey. From the cradle to the cross, He was faithful in His victory walk. Hear Me on this dear one... It was Our joy in the journey of His enduring the cross, despising the shame, to secure your name: My much loved son. My much loved daughter.

"When you grow weary or flagging in your faith, remember this final testimony of true freedom. Let the truth of My Majestic love for you shoot hope straight into your heart. I am your Father and it is My desire to be the freedom for you as you win the race you're in.

"Now, as My Son sits at My right Hand, your freedom is with us. Walk in wisdom and in discernment as you share this truth. I will empower you and strengthen you from the inside out as I inspire you to always do what's right. Your freedom in Me will energize and refresh you as you walk in your healing.

"You will pull on heaven bringing hope and shifting atmospheres. My peace will guide you as you walk in confidence amidst tests and trials. You will not be subject to terror. You will rule over fear. Because you have made Me,

Your Vinedresser, your confidence in times of crisis, I will keep your heart at rest in every situation.

"Rest now here child, with Me as I wrap you with My Presence here in this garden. Put your boxing gloves down. The fight has been won. No matter what the fools or hecklers from the crowd say, the battle for freedom has been accomplished once and for all on the cross. Here lies true freedom. Terror will never conqueror you for I already have.... with My everlasting love.

"So no strive. Simply abide. In the Vine."

Love the Vinedresser

Chapter 3

Beating Fear: Face-Time With Jesus

Read Psalm 16

Fear is like a freight train that runs merciless over you.

Fear slams you against a brick wall breaking bones of faith and taking your breath away.

Fear stamps out the fire of creativity in you.

Fear makes you believe lies....that God does not care and will not help you.

Fear sucks!

If you have felt any of the above, I hope you will read the rest of this chapter

I know I really don't need to focus on fear, and I don't think you do either. But I believe you can defeat it and break it off as you walk in the breaker anointing.

Here is one huge fact. Your spirit is not subject to evil (fear). It is subject to you. Christ in you is the oil (Holy Spirit) that keeps fear from sticking. You are slick...Holy Spirit slick!!!

I've seen fear raise its ugly head recently. It is why I asked the Holy Spirit to help me personally deal with my own issues that can invade my Face-Time with Jesus and mess with the Holy Spirit technology in my heart. (Fun fact: There is no Hebrew word found for the word "presence". In the Psalms, the Hebrew word for it was "face", hence Face-Time with Jesus!)

As Leif Hetland says so well in his book, "Healing The Orphan Spirit-The Father Wants His Kids Back":

"We were created for this kind of encounter—face to face....There is nothing on this earth that could satisfy the longing for the Father's love and embrace."

Recently, one afternoon, as the fear was doing it's best to leave it's foul odor and try to kick me, Holy Spirit lead me to some Scripture which prompted me to write what He was saying.

Tenderly on my heart as I write this are some families dealing bravely with circumstances that could wipe them out with fear.

Close to home, I have a cousin who's wife is going through invasive treatment for cancer. This brings back an album of memories for me as I saw my dad battle the nasty beast in my teens to early 20's. He was brave. He believed God would heal him. As my dad went through chemotherapy and then radiation, his faith never faltered. He NEVER showed signs of fear to his family, although later in life after he passed, I found out he had a few close friends that he leaned on to share his fears.

One thing I did learn from my dad was so simple. Take one day at a time and start the day in the Word. He modeled this all during my young life, before and after the battle with cancer. I have memories of him sitting in this huge green recliner chair reading the Word and praying. He'd pull sheets out of the phone book even and pray over names. I ate my cocoa crispies cereal many a morning observing him before I'd leave for school.

As I was writing this chapter, the Lord directed me to Psalm 16. Will you take some time, get a pen, and read that Psalm? Herein are some major truths to beat any lies of the enemy . You can pour out your heart and let the Word of God put out the fires that fear is trying to cause.

So take the issues that want to smother you with fear and have some Face-Time with Jesus. Keep His Word open in the morning and in your heart through out the day. Not in a striving "I have to do this way", but in intimacy in relationship with your Poppa God.

Here is a declaration and a Word from your Vinedresser:

Declaration: Every day I can have Face-Time with Jesus. In His Presence my heart stays fixed on His love for me which is a fire hydrant to any flames of fear. In His Presence is fullness of Joy!

Listen To The Vinedresser:

"You tell me the smell of fear is all over the place and your heart feels like it will break. I'm glad you can be so honest dear daughter, dear son. Come on in and sit with me in the Vineyard of your heart where you can feel my embrace. Like a soothing balm I will speak love's truth to penetrate your fearful heart.

"Dig deep child! Not in a striving mode but in a resting place. You can hide yourself under the leaves of My PROMISES and abide in My Spirit's coolness from the dew on the grass. Lie down. Let the comfort of My love wrap you like a blanket and take away the coldness of fear you feel.

"Look up! My Spirit reaches to the depth of yours and heaven is united. You pull pools of refreshment from a brook of bliss and the rain of the outpouring splashes out to others. You have authority in Me to speak My peace and alter atmospheres. You are not subject to fear. Fear is subject to you connected here to My Vine!

"Trust Me! You will lack nothing as you walk each day intimately connected to Me, in this Vineyard of your heart. Here lies the rich soil of My Presence to help you grow. I will be generous with My gifts, giving you more than enough...more grace and more glory. Keep walking with integrity and watch Me provide. You will never be in lack as I always have your back.

"It's a process. It's a journey. You are mine. Let go and believe your times are in My Hand. So, don't strive, simply abide, in the Vine."
Love the Vinedresser

Chapter 4

Surviving Internal Pressures

Read Psalm 84

The internal pressures of life do not have to wipe you out. In fact, I know you can be strengthened even while going through heart wrenching situations.

You may be facing betrayal, abuse, control, manipulation or even a death in the family.

I see so many go through this intense struggle and then the result is hearts tattered and broken.

I know it can be easy to fall to the enemy's plot to put you in a pit of self pity.

I heard a good line from my Bethel friend Jenn Stockman about this.

She said, "Self pity wants to steal the five steps to the feet of Jesus."

Jenn Stockman

(Reference to woman who touched Jesus garment and was healed)

But where do you find the purpose amidst this process and not fall into a pit of depression?

I know of only one place...and that is soaking in His Presence being cloaked by His Word.

I'm sharing this Vinedresser word for you with this prayer from Paul. I'm making it my prayer for you.

"For this reason I bow my knees to the Father of our Lord Jesus Christ, from whom the whole family in heaven and earth is named, that He would grant you, according to the riches of His glory, to be strengthened with might through His Spirit in the inner man...."
Ephesians 3:14-16 NKJ

Declaration: I am taking all my cares and burdens and laying them at the feet of Jesus.

Listen to the Vinedresser

"My child, the garden of your heart is becoming dry, cracked, and barren. I see your valiant effort in running the race of your divine designed destiny. Come to Me now, and pour out the disappointment you feel with the delays and heart-aches.

"You can draw from Me purpose in the midst of the internal pressure. Under the surface of your travail lies a spring that My Spirit has deposited in you. Contend with your difficult circumstances by going often to this pool of refreshment. When the world invades your garden with the weeds of worry or foxes of fear, lift up your heart to Me.

"I am your sun. I am your shield. I infuse you with grace and glory. No good thing will I withhold as you walk uprightly. A day in my vineyard is better than thousands in the cesspool of the systems of success based by the world.

"Blessed are you as you dwell in My Vineyard. The garden of your heart is My concern. Now take this time to silently soak. I will sustain you through this intense gardening of your own heart. I will get down on My knees and help you pull the weeds. I will go to the well and pour the water out freely to keep the soil fresh. My Word is the fertilizer that helps you grow.

"Blessed are you as you trust your garden to Me. Your praise produces flowers to replace the wilderness. Your thanksgiving brings the fruit that refresh others. Your garden will reflect the joy of abiding, not striving...in the Vine."

Love the Vinedresser

Chapter 5

Loving Your Self (Soul)

Read Mark 12:28-34

Have you ever thought about the importance of loving your soul. You may think, "Oh come on Theresa, 'He must increase. I must decrease...'"

Well, you can actually stuff your soul in a box and wreak havoc with messed up emotions. I've done that for years so I can speak from experience. So it makes me real excited to share some of the revelation God has given me on this.

What do I really mean by loving your soul?

The answer to that, loving your soul, can be found in context with the greatest commandment of all where Jesus said.

Love the Lord your God with all your heart..

"And you shall love the Lord your God with all your heart, with all your soul, with all your mind, and with all your strength.' This is the first commandment. 31 And the second, like it, is this: 'You shall love your neighbor as yourself.' There is no other commandment greater than these." Mark 12:30-31 NKJ

Let's get real. Think about this. How CAN YOU love your neighbor well, if you are not taking care of your soul?

Soul health. It produces emotional health.

One key of being able to do that is found in declarations. Declare who you are in Him. That you are a carrier of His glory. You are His much loved son, His much loved daughter.

Declarations is one real way to be able to have soul health.

Holy Spirit has been speaking to me about this for quite some time. I realized for so long I had stuffed my soul in the ground. This produced fertile soil for the wrong kind of fruit in the garden of my heart.. Fear dominated with its fruit of anxiety and worry. Ugly fruit. Emotional wrecked fruit.

You don't want that.

So, this is my clue. Love your neighbor AS YOU LOVE YOURSELF.

So, what is something that makes your soul sigh and your heart feels happy?

For me...spending time with my husband just hanging out. I realize I can trust my soul in the embrace of intimacy with Jesus to enjoy activities that are not necessarily "spiritual".

For example, lately my husband and I have watched television series on Netflix. We had gone a good four years without television for various reasons. But in the past few months we have found such great connection with each other, even as we watch different series! We'll see the Father's heart displayed in scenes and give each other high fives. This and various other "coming out of the box" activities of loving my soul has tremendously helped my connection with my main man, my husband.

Another soul love for me is spending time with Kingdom friends. Going out to dinner with other couples, or simply having a cup of coffee with a good friend. This makes my heart so happy and my soul feels like it hums connecting with the "hum" of heaven.

What I mean by this hum is it's that feeling, like after your first sip of coffee in the morning... Or it's the feeling of laying down to take a nap, or going shopping with friends, or that morning walk alone with you and your pet......or...(you fill in the blank.) What makes you sigh in contentment, and it does not have to be something spiritual, but something your body and soul rejoice to experience?

I did write a Vinedresser word. I think it's a tad scattered all over the place type of Word. But that's ok. I'm not into perfection. I'm in to being me. The me God made me. I'm stepping out with no apologies. I'm loving my soul.

Declaration: Soul, you are beautiful, masterly crafted by your God with mass amounts of love. I can trust that my spirit hears my Vinedresser and I am safe in that embrace. I will no longer punish my soul and keep it imprisoned by my body. I am going after the hum of heaven, joyfully expressing my new life in Christ.

Listen To The Vinedresser

"I've got you dear one. I am not trying to kill you. I am healing your soul so you can come into unity with My Spirit. I long to satisfy you fully and bring you back to life. Take your soul out of the box you stuffed it in. Say goodbye to the rotten fruit of fear with its anxiety, judgement, and death to your dreams.

"Your soul is being healed from wounds from sharp arrows of hurt from your past. Your life is no longer driven by fear or rejection. You are spirit driven by Me.

"I see you child as my precious daughter (son). I see you as hand picked by Me to be like my servant Joseph, who was not only the hero of His family, but also a deliverer of many nations.. You are My Kingdom messenger who I love completely, not by what you do, but simply for who you are.

"I made you kind, patient, thoughtful, sensitive, sincere, full of self-control and wisdom as you radiate My Glory. You carry well My Presence to others splashing out My deep love for everyone you meet.

"You hear My Spirit well as you rest in the Secret Place. Your life is a display of My love, revealing jewels of revelation, hope, and peace to others.

"You are being put completely together, body, soul, and spirit, to be a breath of fresh air to the Body, impacting your family and your friends. Your soul is coming alive in true healing as I connect your heart with friends who sharpen you as you sharpen them.

"You can rejoice as you are completely attuned to My Spirit.

"You are a much loved daughter, a much loved son of the King. I am releasing more of My favor on you each day as i raise you up, watch over every step you make, and perfect your soul in my love. You are made in My image with My identity in you. In your spirit identity, you are free to live righteously, love fiercely, and shine with My Glory.

"It's who you are...No strive, simply abide, in the Vine."

Love The Vinedresser .... (lover of your soul)

Chapter 6
24
The Chariot Ride

Psalm 65

He is ready to take you on a chariot ride of love and mercy when:

When the promises of prayers seems slow in coming....

When the no sign of breakthrough is breaking your heart...

When the trauma of the drama is slamming you down...

When the pain is suffocating your hope...

When the noise of emotions from others seems to be drowning out the voice of God!

When the shame makes you go into a lonely isolation state...

I had a prophetic word picture come as I was praying for a precious friend as she was believing God for some real and serious healing to her body. She was still believing but totally worn out from the battle.

As I prayed for this General of the Faith, I saw a picture of a gold chariot. I love this verse found in Psalm 65 in the Passion Translation:

"You crown the earth with its yearly harvest,
the fruits of your goodness.
Wherever you go the tracks of
 your chariot wheels drip with oil."
Psalm 65:11 TPT

I proceeded with a prophetic word for her as I prayed with a vivid picture of God picking her worn body up and placing her gently in his Golden Chariot to take a ride.

I later felt the tug to write a Vinedresser Word from it. She said I could share it with you..

Listen...He is speaking to you..

Declaration: I am not alone. He is taking me on a hope and healing ride in His Presence

Listen To The Vinedresser...

"I see you dear one waiting for the solution to your healing. I hear your heart cry out for your breakthrough. I see you with the present pressures squeezing and suffocating your hope.

"Come near. Let me hold you close with my wrap around Presence. I have a ride waiting for you.

"Let Me pick up your worn body and gently place you in my royal chariot that is decked out with colorful gems sparkling with My colors of love. Sapphires, rubies, My crystals and precious stones reveal that this is My chariot.""

"I want to take you for a ride. Rest here now in the front seat made for comfort as my war horses pull this transportation of hope. Trust in Me.

"Everywhere I take you this chariot leaves tracks of my endless love, dripping oil. Do you feel it. You are getting splashed with the wonderful healing oil of My Spirit. My kindness will not end. My covenant of peace I will keep. Coffee, tea, or simply more of Me is offered.

"This healing victory ride is simply one of many displays of My enduring love for you. As my war horses take you father along the smooth roads displaying My resplendent Glory.....

"The high majestic mountains, the quiet pools of refreshing, the wide green meadows with wild flowers, the valleys filled with fresh clean rivers. Do you see it? Look with the eyes of your heart. This wonder, full of my Presence, is all for you to breath in.

"My love and My mercy will guide you home.

"Now rest child. I will sit in the seat with you, holding you tight. Trust in Me. Rest. Sleep. Watch for more signs of My Presence.

"My war horses know the trails of hope to take, the roads to travel to bring you more of ME with spirit to spirit connections. Yes, these are My much loved sons and daughters who have more of My Heart to sit with you, or to speak prophetic words of My Heart, or simply to listen to you.

"Close your eyes. No striving. Simply abiding in the chariot of My love..... in the vine!"

Love the Vinedresser

Chapter 7

Inner Unity

Psalm 65

Have you ever felt out of joint emotionally.

You know like, something sneaks in, such as doubt and a past failure, and next thing you know you feel like life is draining away from you.

I understand how life's challenges can leave you reeling and slam you down to the ground emotionally.

Is there something you can do that can help eliminate some of these agonizing issues that leave your emotions frayed and your mind fried? Life can become a tight wire walk where you wonder how much more you can take.

Turnaround is a word for you friend. There is a key to walk away from this.

It's this:

I truly believe inner unity, with your soul to your spirit is where your emotions can be restored and even revived. This unity involves identifying what thought or lie is behind the negative emotion.

For example, I used to spend a lot of energy working hard to make money and always focusing on THE MONEY! Simple enough. But in this emotionally charged striving mode all I saw was lack. (I'm not against working hard, by the way.)

How did I adjust this to where now money chases me and I don't chase money?

I simply aligned my soul to my spirit believing the promises that God will supply my needs; that He knows my dreams and visions; and He can perfectly pull it off in greater measures than my wildest dreams.

I am able to trust the dream. I don't have to make it happen as I work from peace. I trust the supernatural. God is for me and desires to see me living out of my true identity, in **HIM!**

My core belief behind this is I know God has set me on a course of providing not only media training but also prophetic coaching. I help Kingdom Messengers, like you, discover your true identity so you can have the resources to be successful in your call.

The problem happens when you dwell or look for evidence in your mind of what does not line up with this belief.

Let me candidly give you an example. I had applied for a part-time social media job recently for a brilliant Kingdom ministry that I thought would be awesome to help.

I did not get the job. As I read the email I had a choice to make. I could use this as a building block to a negative emotion of "failure", or I could align my thoughts to my core belief based on what God has said to me. (And, I might add, what my husband has prophetically said to me not to apply and just walk in the lane God has given as a Kingdom leader carrying the Father's heart and a Mentor in the media field.)

My core belief? I know He has equipped me to make a difference in people like you with Kingdom mentoring on identity and Kingdom media for spreading your message.

Here is the catch.

Your mind (soul) is looking for evidence of that which you think you don't have or can't do.

What do you do?

Identify the core belief that is opposite of receiving God's best for you in that area. Many of our false beliefs have created the wrong conclusions from past soul wounds. Your negative thoughts can be what's triggering the very things you want to receive. Declarations are crucial of what God says.

You can walk in soul health. That means loving yourself and taking care of your self; soaking in many baths in the warm water of what God says (declarations); immersing your soul wounds with the soothing truth of God's majestic love for you; walking in forgiveness always and staying away from offense.

What's amazing as this inner unity with your spirit and soul becomes a reality, your body aligns with it. Hence, healing comes to you physically, spiritually, and yes emotionally.

The Vinedresser had something to say for you about this...with a declaration.

Declaration: I can trust my life in God's Hand. Hope and rest are my companions as I take care of my self and align my spirit with my soul. I listen to my spirit and trust it can be lead by Christ's Spirit. He is within me. I am His garden of delight.

Listen to the Vinedresser

"Dear child you can jump off the performance merry-go-around into my loving arms here in this intimate place. Sit down close next to me in this private oasis, deep down the rows of this garden and receive my revelation-secrets that are loaded with promises for you.

"I offer a resting place for you to bask in the Son of my luxurious and never fading love. I long for you to come into inner unity of your soul with your spirit. I long to help you restore your emotions and revive your life.

"Do not dwell on your failures which rob you of hope and sap the life out of you. Spend time with Me and let me whisper more love secrets and faith filled promises. Let me heal your soul so your can believe completely that I have your life in My Hands.

"As you come into this inner unity you with your spirit and your soul, you are set free to dance and live in your true identity. Your spirit is meant to fly in the design I have placed in your very DNA. You are meant to live energized and motivated to soar even higher, not in striving but abiding.

"Choose to dwell on what I say about you. I will restore complete soul health so you can be emotionally free. Be real with me Child. Soak your soul wounds in My love for healing. I am for you. Get so lost in love with Me. Experience victory in your true identity in my embrace. So no striving, simply abiding in the Vine."

Love the Vinedresser

Chapter 8

Turnaround In Your Health

Read Isaiah 53

I wrote a prophetic word recently which contained three parts..

The word contained the thoughts of turnaround involving a shift in changing your belief system, to eviction notice to fear and then to seeing your most deepest heart needs, hopes and dreams becoming a reality.

So, how about you getting a word for your turnaround health?

Allow me to bring a testimony for your own breakthrough.

Toward the late part of one year recently, I struggled with some unexpected health issues, one in particular that was border line been life threatening. As I thought about this, I realized something very profound.

I was able to go through the pain with much peace. A foundation of being loved by God, knowing my identity, and having my husband and close friends' compassion made this time of anguish bearable. We are designed by

God to be loved and in community. That force can help you through so many difficult situations.

So, I challenge you to get a word from Holy Spirit now for your health. I'm not just talking your physical health but also your soul health.

How do you do this? Well, God will speak to you and I can bet it will be full of HIS Word and His promises. I love what Joaquin Evans of Bethel's Healing Rooms said one night at class at school (Bethel Atlanta School of The Supernatural)..

"The assignment is to release love encounters with God. If you are having people having love encounters with God, the sick will get healed."—Joaquin Evans

Love encounters. I believe this is the key. And it is one I am using as a foundation for my "word" concerning my physical and soul health.

You can adopt this word and add to it, if you like.

So I have been pursuing and looking for love encounters with Holy Spirit. One morning I ended up spending two hours simply soaking in the Word of God.

Filling up with His love first in any day sets a foundation to walk as God has designed you to walk. It also is a great help amidst speed bumps and sharp curves along the process of life.

I hit a curve already this year. It took a day of worshiping (while I watched my husband work laying down a tile floor) to manage my way through the tangled emotions. Instead of staying in a pit of rejection or other emotional throw up for weeks, I asked God humbly to speak to me. He did...through my husband and a few close friends.

Your "God need" to be loved can have a direct relationship with your health!

Check this quote:

"A deep sense of love an belonging is an irreducible need of all people. We are biologically, cognitively, physically, and spiritually wired to love, to be loved, and to belong. When those needs are not met, we don't function as we were meant to. We break. We fall apart. We numb. We ache. We hurt others. We got sick." Brene Brown.

So, a big part of this Word for my health from the Lord does not only have to do with my physical needs but also my soul needs.

So I activate the declarations of what God says as I say "no" to fear (or the enemies lies), and continue walking in the destiny God has laid out for me.

How do I say this word now? Let me see if a declaration and a word from the Vinedresser will help me out and maybe encourage you.

Declaration: I am lovable. I receive love and receive healing. I am walking and declaring divine health over my body, my mind, my soul...my life!!

Listen to the Vinedresser:

"I am your lover, your friend. Walk with Me and experience the healing love of being connected to Me, child. My Son has carried your weaknesses, your illnesses, even your greatest needs. From the bloody cross to the cold tomb, He made the way for the ultimate in healing grace. The price has been paid.

"I do not train through pain. Your desire for love, belonging, and being loved is from Me. I wired your internal needs for being loved and being connected for significance. So connect with Me in the Vine. I am the same yesterday, today, and forever. I am the only One who will never let you down. Do you know what that means to you? I still like to heal bodies. I still like to see you laugh with friends. I still heal marriages and family relationships.

"Bring your battered and torn heart and body to me. Lean against My arms.

"I will hold you and make you whole. Immerse yourself in Me as I bathe you with the cool mist of My Presence. I will hold your hand with tenderness as you lay on your healing bed, or feel an arrow of rejection. I will kiss your heart and make it whole. My divine health and healing is here. Your greatest pleasure will be in My loving you and you abiding with Me.. in the Vine."

Love the Vinedresser

Chapter 9

Zipping Fear

Read Psalm 27

Zipping fear on a zip line.

What do I mean?

Well, I will tell you there are many chapters in this devotional on beating fear. So I hope this helps you in your journey. This one lesson was like no other in facing my fears.

Recently I joined a gang of Jesus loving sisters who decided to celebrate a friend's birthday by going to the mountains where a course of zip lines were set up for recreation. (Definition: consists of a pulley suspended on a cable... It is designed to enable a user to propel by gravity to travel from one end of a location by a long cable by holding on to another by a the freely moving pulley.)

This is what I discovered.

I was racked with fear in the beginning as we put on our gear while the instructor gave instructions of how this "fun" happens.

The saving grace was being around my friends who faced these pre-zipping fears with lots of nervous laughter.

To start, we had to cross this shaky bridge to get to the platform of this first line to zip.

Trust. We had to trust our equipment, instructors, and the line itself to hold us and work to keep from falling down to the ground.

There is something about running and jumping off that platform and then zipping down that wire that brought pure joy to my soul.

We spent the next hour cheering each other on as we tackled each zip line....or like me, tackled the instructor who had to catch me as I forgot to "break".

One friend wrote later:

"It was quite the life-changing, girl-bonding, knee-shaking good time! Even though it was scary as heck, I wouldn't have missed out on an adventure with these chicks..."

What am I trying to say?

Will Smith said it like this:

"God places the best things in life on the other side of terror."

Sometimes our mind creates a greater fear than the reality of what we are facing. I was the most nervous while getting my helmet and awkward gear strapped on. As I did this my thoughts raced with terror of the what if's...What if this breaks...what if I fall...etc. Those fears melted away as I trusted the equipment in mid-air to support me, to my thrill seeking satisfaction.

What are you fearing?

May I remind you...37

You are designed and meant to fly. No ropes. You are meant to soar in the designs and frequencies of heaven in your spirit identity.

Will you believe in the support system of the Holy Spirit? The equipment of faith? The helmet of your salvation? The belt of truth around your waste?

I pray this word from the Vinedresser will soothe those jagged edges of your nerves that have wreaked havoc in your life with fear.

I see you flying....and trusting... Smile friend, He has you!

Declaration: I can trust God that He has my life in His hands. I will not fear but trust Him as I walk away from fear and into His arms of love.

Listen to the Vinedresser

"Dear child. That monster of fear that has been chasing you for so long is defeated. When your heart feels like its raging with trepidation, draw nearer and deeper into My garden. Let me calm you.

"Let me love You where panic has ravaged your heart and where your emotions have been on a merry-go-round going way too fast. Soak in the peaceful pool of My tender love. My Spirit is gentle to cleanse your wounds from trauma that tries to take up residence in your heart.

"Come now into this Vineyard and experience My Presence. Here you can feel the gentle beats of My heart as I hold you close. My love is stronger than these chains of horror. I am the fire and light inside of you. I will never leave you in the dark or out in the cold. Fear with its fruit of pain and persecution will never quench the raging fire of love I lit inside of you.

"I am near. My love will capture you and you will never be the same. Watch how I can bring back what the enemy has stolen. Join the parade of My lovers rejoicing and dancing in the streets of freedom.

"Do you hear that? It's time for you to rejoice My love. You can join the chorus and sing 'My Father is the King of My heart...My Father loves me....He is a good ather...'

"Yield to My furious and unrelenting love. Your faith in My majestic love makes you hell's furry. The enemy has no power over you. You are not a friend of fear. You are a friend of Me.

"Your breakthroughs of squashing your agitation of worry makes you a carrier of My Presence, helping others to do the same around you. Remember now... No performance needed child. No strive but abide....in the Vine."

Love the Vinedresser

Chapter 10

God Says.. Turnaround

James 1

I like to write what Holy Spirit says...any time He speaks.

Right now? He is saying:

"Hold on. Hold tight. I'm not finished what I started in you. The process is for relationship, so draw closer to Me as I work on your behalf. You simply remember you are coming from a position of victory, from heaven. You have My Spirit in you. So no feelings of "stalls", "letdowns", "crisis", or "attack" is greater than Me. You are not subject to evil. It's subject to you. This is the year of turnaround. Will you take My Hand and walk by faith in between the now and the not yet?"

What dreams and hopes and visions have you been waiting on to manifest?

The last part of a prophetic word I received for this one year had to do with this statement: This will be "your year" to see the birth of hopes and dreams you have been pregnant with for so long.

God says: Breakthrough. Turnaround. He is slapping His favor on you and your family by your obedience!

So many people talk about breakthrough...And how badly they need one in their finances, marriage or circumstance.

I asked Holy Spirit about this. Part of what He said was in this Vinedresser word.. Maybe this

will HELP YOU this year.

I am writing this as a Vinedresser word again.

Why do I do this?

Well this time, I have felt quite "dry" these past few weeks. The battle is intense after a car wreck. My hope is still high. My faith has not wavered. But... I won't make up things to write just because the "ink in my pen" is low.

So, I'll leave you with this declaration and word in hopes you may be encouraged.

Declaration: I believe in a God of turnarounds. My turnaround is here. I will trust and rest in Him.

Listen to the Vinedresser

"Beloved, stand back and look with the eyes of your heart. Your wounds and heart cares are what your mind sees, but you can supersede reality with the eyes of magnificent faith. Can you see it?

"I open a door before you that no one can slam shut. This open door leads to the brooks far in this vineyard full of refreshing sweet revelation. You can rest your weary body here and lay your hurts and offenses down from family or those who do not know your tender heart.

"Focus not on the pretenders whose true membership is in the club of the enemy. You cannot fight to take ground from the enemy if he has found ground in you with offenses you hold. Don't look at those who mock and speak evil of you.

"The majesty of My love for you will confront their pretensions and they will acknowledge it's you who I've set my love on. Did you hear that child. It's you who I have set my everlasting love on.

"You see beloved, I rejoice how you have kept My Word in such diligent and passionate patience. I delight in walking you through the tedious process of breakthrough.

"It's here, in this process, which makes me joyful knowing you will pass each test. Keep a tight grip on Me beloved, I am here. I will keep you safe in your time of testing. The only breaking that will happen will be your breakthrough. The door is open now. Come dwell and be the breakthrough. No strive. Simply abide.. in the Vine."

Love the Vinedresser

Chapter 11

Healing Shattered Hearts

Song of Songs 1:6-9

I was praying and rewriting a Vinedresser word the Holy Spirit gave me after I came back staying at a Christian retreat center where a couple of precious friends work.

One afternoon, the Holy Spirit spoke a loud word in my spirit, amidst the demands I witnessed on the work needed to be done there. This word simply washed over my heart.

He said clearly: "I am more concerned with healing shattered hearts that I am in the success of a ministry".....

It struck a deep cord in my heart. I know these past few years have been a process for me to learn that God does not want my performance or my "work ethic" to please Him. (Don't get me wrong a work ethic is good but not in trying to please God). He just wants my heart. His desire is to hold me, which molds me. He is teaching me to rest in his affections reminding me who I am: a much loved daughter of the King.

When it comes to this PBA (performance based acceptance with striving), I am often reminded of the Shulamite in the Song of Songs. She was put to work by her brothers as an appointed minister of "their ministry vineyards." (Read in Chapter 1 in the Passion Translation) She realized they were draining her and the care of her own heart was left unattended.

I can relate that often in the name of "ministry" I easily become all Martha with no Mary in my pursuit of perfection in my work. That is what this declaration and Listen to the Vinedresser is all about.

Whether you are in ministry or not, I pray you will not get snared by the yoke of religion......and find FREEDOM in who God says you are!

Declaration: God does not want my performance but my devotion to Him. I am His delight. My life carries the aroma of His grace.

Listen To The Vinedresser

"Dear child, sometimes creating a safe boundary means you have to let go. Your heart is a delicate garden meant to display the fruits of your devotion to Me, not to anyone or anything the world has to offer.

"I know how you desire to work and work to please others or to walk out demands in performance. In that place you neglect the care of the Vineyard within. Listen. There is no performance based acceptance going on from Me. I love you for you, period.

"Now take my Hand of grace...This indescribable gift of grace. Be yoked with me. Be entwined in the Vine. Here we can walk the rows together and experience sweet moments of intimacy as the sun rises. I am here to dance with you as the sun finds its place of setting. Your tattered and worn heart can be refreshed in the pools of My gentle love.

"Watch how this simple walk with me will energize other parts of your being. I unlock the combination of your heart so you have no need to remember some random number. I then give you the key that is accessible every moment of every day to rest in My Vineyard and restore your soul.

"So, come now my dear radiant child, follow in My footsteps where I lead My lovers. Drop your burdens and worries and come to the place where you will always find Me. I am here to refresh your heart and enhance your beauty. You resemble My redeeming grace and your devotion brings a sweet fragrance of praise. The Vineyard of your heart is pleasing to Me, a true anointed resting place, a perfect home.

"So dear one, continue to soak, continue to blossom in the shade of My Love. Rest in My delight where My glory never fades. Remember this is not in striving but simply abiding...in the Vine."

Love the Vinedresser

Chapter 12

Pushing Back Anxiety

Read 1 Peter 5:6-10

Can you really deal with and conquer your anxiety?

Yes, you can as you build on your spirit identity. Guess what? This is not something you work at but a shift into believing what God says about you! With this shift, comes the breaker anointing!

I've been very persistent in asking God to help me walk this spirit identity out in relation to worry. I've had my struggles.

I remember this time one morning a few years where I was really fighting anxiety. I have been walking in great peace and joy lately so this was quite disturbing to me. Even though it was election Tuesday, I still could not quite pin point the source of the angst I felt. I thought maybe I was feeling it for my husband or a friend. Even though I know part of my prophetic gift deals heavily with what I feel in the atmosphere, I still could not shake it.

I was in a place where I could not process this with anyone as my husband was busy at work and a few friends were out of reach. I'm rather glad now that I had no one but the

Holy Spirit to work through this. As I was processing with it, the Holy Spirit spoke this to me:

"You can push back the anxiety you feel by pressing into my Presence. The press comes as you shift your MIND and activate your Spirit to hear from ME. It's a spirit-identity shift. You can ask Me for more..... what ever you need...healing, peace, finances, connections. I delight to take good care of My children."

So, I was asking Him for the shift from anxiety to my spirit identity. I wrote out some declarations for myself based on Scripture.

No relief.

I got up and went on a minor cleaning spurt. Even got on my knees to mop the floor of my laundry room. I just felt like maybe being busy cleaning (and pleasing my husband) might help me shake the heavy gorilla resting on my heart. (chuckle).

Finally I sat down and simply tried to enter His Presence. I had read a lot of the Word that morning so I pondered what I had read looking for a slight point of understanding to my anxiety. Soaking in the word is a great set up to hear His Voice.

As sure as the wind started to gently blow the leaves on the trees outside my window, I knew I could ask Holy Spirit for a word from the Vinedresser for me. So I went over the declarations I had written and started to write in the voice of my Lord, Friend, Comforter, The Vinedresser.

I am so thankful for the Holy Spirit. His Words break off the fear that wants to produce it's bad fruit of anxiety.

You can do this too. Stay in the Word. Be sensitive to the Holy Spirit. See with your Spirit eyes, from your heart, not your physical side from your mind. God speaks to your Spirit-heart, not your mind. Take note of what stirs up negative emotions or forces by different places or situations.

Instead of falling to a victim mentality, rise up seeing yourself carrying the very presence of God and emanating His love, peace, and favor everywhere you go. I believe this inward conscious walk will bring shifts in your atmosphere as you carry His Presence.

As you learn to walk this way, being more sensitive to your spirit, you begin to understand you are in Christ, living in a place of habitation. You are seated with Him at God's right Hand. As you continue to abide in Him, you can experience a total overhaul of your identity of who you really are. You can remind yourself that God is in control. You have no need trying to manage other people. He is the Mediator!

So ready? Let's make a declaration.

Declaration: I can conquer anxiety because I am one with Him. He lives in me. I can live by the Spirit Wind in peace and confidence. I carry His breaker anointing.

Listen To The Vinedresser

"My child, check the troubled beats of your heart with this word. You are Spirit born. Cast off the anxiety that wants to eat away your true identity and focus on My Words. You are born from above. The Presence of My Glory is swirling and dancing all around you. Do you feel the substance of this Spirit Wind?

"Rejoice dear one, for you are seated perfectly in heavenly places in Me. Soak up the Spirit substance of My radiant splendor and deep peace I have for you. Like a piece of cornbread dipped in a big glass of milk, so I thoroughly immerse you with My virtue and divine love.

"You are a Spirit being having a human experience making a great spiritual impact everywhere I choose to lead you. Soak in Me. This is like a piece of cornbread dipped in a big glass of milk. So I long to thoroughly immerse you with my virtue and divine love.

"Reach in with your heart, not your mind, and experience deep into the very core of your cells this cleansing and freeing love. I am in you. You carry the essence and aroma of being face to face with Me. You are meant for this Spirit identity. Watch it grow from intimacy with Me. You will be the one radiating My Presence as I show you how to release healing, and deliverance to people. Your Spirit will hum as you hear My Voice speak to you about the majestic love I have for everyone from which I lead you to speak.

"You glow resplendently with My light, peace, and love. You carry My grandeur into places of darkness, deceit, and disease from the enemy. Your Spirit will be quickened with excitement as I lead you to demolish sickness, break the chains of bondage, and spring free the captives.

"Watch evil and wickedness flee because of the indwelling of My Spirit in and upon you. You effortlessly exude radical manifestations of My power, not by your own effort, but simply because you are a laid down lover of Me.

"So walk on in My Spirit, beloved, from a place of victory. No need for you to strive. Simply stay in My Presence and abide as you bring heaven to earth.

Love the Vinedresser

Chapter 13

My Lips Shall Praise You

Read Song of Songs 4

I have had times of dealing with very severe chapped lips. I woke up one morning feeling like the lower lip was laser burned.

As I did a google search to find a remedy, I asked the Lord the physical manifestation of something spiritual coming out of my life.

What words have I spoken out of my own fear or hurt? How have I betrayed trust by what I might have said?

Tough questions, for sure.

So I continued on in my journey soaking in the Song of Songs. Instantly I found truths to what I was praying.

The first thing that I did was ask the Lord for forgiveness. I find my words can be the most cutting with those who I live with in my home. I don't want this to be. I want my family to get the first fruit coming from my lips with words of mercy, grace, and love. I desire my words to be an oasis of clean fresh water to wash their wounds and speak life over their issues. I desire to be the calm amidst a heart storm.

Makes sense but I had this thought for you.

What if YOU are the one enduring cutting words from those around you? How do you make sense from words that spew out drama and trauma leaving your heart feeling like it's shred into pieces?

I'm sorry for the intense wounding this can bring. It is challenging but I believe you can be the one to look into HIS eyes of love which produces a sweetness out of your mouth. From the travail of your heart comes the wisdom to be a buffer of grace from the drama of the trauma in words for yourself and those close around you.

I asked the Vinedresser to help speak to you about this. This is what HE said with a declaration.

Declaration: My lips shall praise Him. I walk in purity as I speak this truth: I know my Lover is mine, and I have everything in HIM, for we delight ourselves in each other.

Listen To The Vinedresser

"I'm looking into your eyes dear lover of Mine. As we enter this intimate place in My Vineyard, My love soaks the wear and tear of your bruised heart. Allow Me to be a banner of healing over you as I gently take the arrows out, and soak your brutal bruises in My warm liquid love.

"Now hide yourself deep down in this garden where you can hear only My voice. The cooing of the doves and the fragrance of daisies are whispering intimate words of My love, faithfulness, and grace over your life. Rest here in the cleft of this row in My Vineyard as I speak gently with mercy how you can grow in deeper devotion with Me.

"So dear one, I'm calling you to arise from your performance in self and break off the chains of introspection that brings distance from Me. We can do this together as we catch the foxes of fear that hinder our relationship. Fear that spews out in words that are laser sharp which wounds hearts, yours and others around you.

"Do this for Me, my Beloved.

"Listen to this! My love does not cease even amidst your process of walking in My ways. I do not see a child tripping and falling. I see a much loved son learning to walk in His true identity. I do not see a dear daughter clamoring for attention. I see a much loved daughter attending to her heart for purity.

"You are everything My Son died for to make you Mine.

"I hear you! I am attentive to your cries for help. Do you know your voice is sweet and pleasing to Me? Your prayers are a magnificent sound in My ears. Your loving words to Me are sweeter than honey. Your intercession is a wonderful note of music.

"So say this dear lover of Mine!

"'I know my Lover is mine, and I have everything in you, for we delight ourselves in each other.'

"Yes! That is the truth for you to walk confidently forward in your journey. I will continue to travel close with you in this Vineyard, feeding you more deep things of My heart so you can walk in pureness in words and action.

"You are my lover. I give you everything as we delight in each other...In this garden of no striving, simply abiding...in the Vine."

Love the Vinedresser

Amazing what chapped lips will reveal. (chuckle)

Chapter 14

A True Valentine Love

Read 1 Corinthians 12:12 thru 1 Corinthians 13

For chapter 14, how about some thoughts on your relationship in the Vine, connections with Jesus, and true valentine love?

Recently after an auto wreck, filled with long hours of doctor visits (for Dave), I was thinking of connections, meaning THE connection in relation to Father God.

So while I am sitting in a Chic-fil-a with two moms and their kids sitting (loudly) over from me, I tried to remember what Holy Spirit said the day before.... It was so awesome. But I had no computer to write what He said down.

Bummer.

What was God saying yesterday?

What is the ultimate of connection?

This came to mind:

All of you together are Christ's body, and each of you is a part of it. 1 Corinthians 12:27

So the ultimate connection is being one with Jesus. Out of that flows the life source for us to live in our Spirit identity and to be an agent of God's love. As He grafts you in the Vine, you carry the very DNA of Jesus to impact hearts for heaven!!

So, since Valentines day is coming up, I went searching the Word for some true Valentine love thoughts .

I'll simply end this with a Vinedresser Word which He spoke days later on a trip home from a prison visit near the Florida State line. While I rarely type on my computer going down the road, the worship music and company with one who has showed me true valentine love, my husband, seemed just the best intimate place to connect with you.

So, this is just for you, friend. The Holy Spirit let me feel the exhaustion and frustration that you are in now in terms of connections. It might be a spouse who lets you down or a friend who betrayed your trust. Get a cup of coffee (or tea) and let the Vinedresser speak healing words of love to your soul.

Declaration: I am my His Valentine and I dine in the Vine on His love every day. He loves me.

Listen To The Vinedresser

"Dear Valentine...don't you know how much I love you? My devotion to you is written in red by the blood of My Son. In this redeeming love, I have placed greatness in you as I deliver you from the cesspool of your searching for love apart from Me. So now, let Me Kiss your heart with forgiveness so true healing can help you be balanced and complete. I give you the Key to My heart for access day and night.

"Here, lover of Mine, pick my flowers of faithfulness that carry the aroma of My glory wrapping around your tender heart. You may not receive flowers from your loved one here on earth, but I always have a bouquet of My Presence to lavish on you. Your unrelenting worship of Me, even amidst arrows to your soul, produces My sweeter than wine love whispers. Let me flood your very being with a torrential love, like a river overflowing its banks with kindness and mercy.

"Do you know what I see when I look into your eyes? I see your radiant beauty. I'm held captive by your passion. Your undying devotion to Me makes my heart skip a beat as the hosts of heaven stand at attention in awe. Lovely even in your weakness, I see you as My strong tower bringing the very DNA of Me, as My breaker anointing messenger, impacting thousands of hearts for heaven.

"You are without equal, the perfect beloved dove for Me, crowned as royalty. I cannot even count the delights you bring Me. Truly your love is the greatest as I get to feast in your vineyard of love. You truly are the one who brings Me bliss. Let's continue to dance close together as I spin you forward with all the strength and power you need. Lose yourself in My love now dear one and allow My glory to consummate the fullness of My Love for you, fulfilling your heart's desires. So, no strive now, simply abide, in My Presence, in this Vineyard of love."

Love your Valentine, the Vinedresser

Chapter 15

Steps To Turn Around

Read Hebrews 2

I received a great question on my Facebook page the other day. The question: "Can a turnaround from the Lord be slow... In steps... or not all at once?"

It's a great question. In my experience with hearing from the Holy Spirit, I believe it can be both.

For example, a friend of mine received a complete turnaround recently. He had to wait for it, but there was no doubt it was a dramatic move of God's favor and a complete turnaround.

I also believe your turnaround can happen in steps. God is all about the process so some turnarounds come step by step. I understand you sometimes wonder when your breakthrough will happen. I'm sorry the process can throw you down and crush your heart at times.

Yes, I know you are more than ready for your turnaround.. in your family, in your marriage, in your finances, in your.........you fill in the blank.

I believe this question is a key for you to experience your turnaround and trust Him amidst the process:

How engaged are you in the truths of the Word and walking them out with declarations?

"This is why it is so crucial that we be all the more engaged and attentive to the truths that we have heard so that we do not drift off course." Hebrews 2:1 tpt

I know in my heart being engaged in His Word, and actively walking out my faith are just some of the steps for a turnaround and a huge key to reign in life. So my heart is bent to not merely read the Words but walk them out in my belief system, by my actions, faith and declarations.

The woman who asked the question was believing for a dramatic turnaround in her health. My heart went out to her. I also have been persistent in prayer for some close friends for their turnaround. As I cry out, He speaks...with a declaration and a word from the Vinedresser:

Declaration: I believe for my turnaround now. I know God holds me close and is working all things for good. I love Him and trust Him with this process. He is my hope and my deliverer.

Listen to the Vinedresser

"I see you in the travail of your pain right now. You have grasped tightly to my truths and walked them out. Your suffering is bringing out the gold. How My heart rejoices to see you walk in the path of My Son Jesus, giving it all to Me.

"I didn't leave Jesus hanging on the cross. So I won't leave you dangling, wondering if I will come through for you. Listen child, run into my heart; the gate is wide open into My Vineyard. i will stop at nothing to heal your shattered heart and your aching soul. Faithfulness, strength, comfort, and joy is all in My Presence. I see you dear one. Your gut wrenching moment is not hidden from My eyes.

"Walk on and see how I will empower you to seize the fulfillment of My promises in your life, in your family, in your destiny. I have established this all ahead of time child.

"I'm giving you an unshakeable hope and never ending glory. Like a strong, huge, unbreakable anchor thrown out into the stormy seas of your life tsunami, you can hope in Me.

"For I am in the wild wind, the dark clouds, the freezing faith times of your life. This anchor of hope is tightly fastened to the mercy seat of My unshakable love radiating to you from the heavenly realm.

"This love I have for you. It distinguishes the fear. It sets the lost free. It breaks the chains. It softens hearts. It brings answers to your prayers. It helps make sense amidst the madness. Keep reaching for Me in worship. Feel My Presence in the wind. Listen to My intimate love songs that only you can hear.

"Hide yourself in this garden of My faithfulness. No strive in the moment. Simply abide in My canopy of love.. abide...in the Vine."

Love the Vinedresser

Chapter 16

Beating Barriers To Your Dreams

Read Exodus 4:27-29

Beating the barriers to your dreams starts now. Yes, your fears are often your roadblocks.

I get that.

What if I told you there is one key to really beat fear and propel you forward?

Love. Choose His love and let Him take your from fried, tried, and crucified to love which holds, molds and creates you to be the "perfect you" which God has designed before time.

By the way, I still believe in turnaround for you. He gave you the dreams. Now is the time for acceleration.

How? By breaking the barriers of fear.

Pain and disappointment are some of the barriers to breakthrough.

Good news. You have a choice to love and trust Him. You have a choice to not isolate yourself and receive healing amidst the context of community and Kingdom family.

Here is a truth to hang your hope hat on:

God cares.

As I was reading the Word recently, this one verse stuck out. The Israelites were in their own battle against the Egyptians who were literally and figuratively working them to death. After 40 years of process in the desert, God sent Moses back to them with hope.... and then..

"Then the people of Israel were convinced that the Lord had sent Moses and Aaron. When they heard that the Lord was concerned about them and had seen their misery, they bowed down and worshiped." Exodus 4:31 NLT

May I remind you the Lord is concerned about you. He has keys for you to move from misery into living messages of hope for others. He has not forgotten your desires and dreams!

The struggle is not your norm. As you walk in your spirit identity can learn to flourish in the midst of the trials and resistance. You are able to worship while you wait.

What is the position of trust when the waves seem to be crashing you into the sand. You get up with sand in your mouth only to be pushed down again. You're wet. Your tired. Your body even aches from the slam.

FLOAT!

God told me this is the time to float. It involves trust. Let Him hold you and carry you. Trust. Choose to focus on

HIM and not the waves crashing in on you. That trust word is an action word.

So, in that choice is a place of faith and worship to declare HE loves you, and He won't let you drown. Beating the barriers to destiny means keeping the declarations alive and spoken out of your mouth.

I wrote this Vinedresser Word to encourage you to embrace HIM amidst the yuck of your life. I pray it encourages you.

Declaration: I CHOOSE to trust that God cares for me. I choose Him. I choose love.

LISTEN To The Vinedresser

"When you're hurt, devastated and trauma has taken its toll, run hard deep into the garden to receive my embrace of grace. I am here. Choose Me and hold Me and drop the rock of offense in your hand. In My embrace you can face this shattering pain and find the ammunition to kill your dashed hopes and dreams.

"I give you this choice. Choose Me and choose life. I have given you so many precious and magnificent promises to power you through the minefield of your setbacks and delays in your destiny. My word will bring purpose amidst the wait. My promises are always yes and amen. I have your times in My hands.

"You can choose what I say and be healed from the foxes of fear that have wrecked havoc in your mind. I give you life, and life more abundant. In Me lies the power to walk in the perfect you I have created you to be.

"I have wired you for love and greatness in My Kingdom. You have a song that only you can sing that comes straight from My heavenly courts. You have a message from the mess of trespassed abuse from your past that will set others free to fly like you.

"So walk on through the process my precious child. It's in the process and the waiting that you find that spot in the garden of your heart where My voice speaks clearly. My voice drowns out the toxic thoughts that come from the fear that has been running after you, tripping you up with each direction you take.

"I am near to heal your ravished and overwhelmed heart. The branches in this Vineyard will hold you close as I wrap my arms and hold you close to My heart. Listen to the cadence of the beat of My heart that sings over you...songs of love....songs of deliverance...songs of hope.

"You can choose to soak in My Vineyard. In My Presence is fullness of joy. You are meant to live on top of the mountain, not under it. Speak often My Promises over your life.

"Now lay down your pride and remember: NO performance needed. No strive. Simply abide."
Love the Vinedresser

Chapter 17

Dealing With Pain And Trauma

Read Psalm 18

Sometimes you have to learn through your own pain and sickness on how to deal with it.

I have recently shared in my Spirit Identity Series Video/Book how my soul and body reacts to trauma. I hope my candid sharing here might help you as you learn to walk in your spirit identity. (You are a spirit being having a human experience.)

So, recently I had the following events happen:

One night on the way home from school (Bethel Atlanta School of The Supernatural) with Dave driving, we came across a doe crossing over our lane. "Look! Deer!" says Dave!

And then the next thing I know I'm staring into the eyes of a six point buck coming right at me in my front windshield. Dave was amazing, steering clear just in time, as I felt the Buck's antlers scrape my side of the little car.

Just to remind you if you didn't know, Dave and I were just in a wreck at the beginning of the year, so 10 months later this feeling is all too familiar. I called 911. Got transferred three times. We eventually went home and a State Patrol came to our home and wrote up a report.

Then, the next morning, I awake to a phone call from Dave who had left early for work.

"Theresa, I'm in a wreck. Gotta call 911." (By the way, he is ok after this accident)

I got the same kind of call in January of 2013 when Dave was in a massive wreck and God spared his life.

Well, I woke up a one morning after Dave's recent wreck to excruciating pain with a bladder infection.

You are asking, "What happened?" Right?

I'm learning a lesson. As I talked with Dave, I realized my hyper stressed feelings were not being dealt with and fear brought an ugly affect, trauma, to my soul.

I know God does not like to see His children in pain.

This verse made me feel like God was holding my heart in Psalm 118.

"When I was at my weakest, my enemies attacked—
But the Lord held on to me.
His love broke open the way
And he brought me into a beautiful broad place.
He rescued me—because his delight is in me!"
Psalm 18:18-19 tpt

(Read Psalm 18 in the Passion Translation for more insight)

I remembered how God showed me the reality of His deep love for me right before Dave's wreck. At church a precious woman of God had given me a prophetic word written out...at the end it had this verse:

"The Lord your God in your midst,
The Mighty One, will save;
He will rejoice over you with gladness,
He will quiet you with His love,
He will rejoice over you with singing."
Zephaniah 3:17 (NKJV

So amidst all this pain, I actually heard ANGELS singing over me in the middle of the night. For real, like I heard them.!! It was so awesome as I've asked Him to speak to me at night, in my dreams.

So, I'm not going to let a crash dash my hopes and visions.

No matter the battering of your soul or your body, you always have a healer who helps you walk in health. It matters to Him. You carry great value. He's all about mending wounds of our soul keeping us away from the drama of the trauma.

The Vinedresser had a word with a declaration that I think is perfect NOW to share.

So here's a healing declaration:

Declaration: I can walk in soul health and be healed of any infirmity. I am a spirit being who is having a healthy human experience.

Listen to the Vinedresser:

"Do you hear Me singing over you as you lay on your sick bed in pain? I am your healer, dear one and I'm singing songs of sweet revelation in tongues of angels. Lay your heart in My arms. I am an oasis of peace and mighty deliverer. I give you rest for your body and soul.

"Listen dear child. I do not train through pain. Your desire for recovery is my desire. It's okay to question the why's. But, beloved, clear the way in your soul for all of My promises. For I know the great plans I have for you. Yes, plans for your welfare, your health, and not evil. I am here to give you a restored future and a rejuvenated hope.

"Make your declarations on My promises, which are yes and amen, in my Son.

"So, say yes to mending bodies from affliction. Yes, to eyes being open to see; restoring of ears to hear. Yes to limbs growing, cancer cells annihilated, and blood sugar levels normal. My Son has carried your weaknesses, has been beaten and crushed . The price has been paid.

"Do you know what that means to you? I am the same yesterday, today, and for ever. These are not facts for your brain but truths for your heart that rescue you from the pit of despair. Bring your battered and torn body to me. Lean against My arms as I take you out of the chaos and draw you to Myself.

"No matter the depths of anguish you feel, I will rescue you because I delight in you. I will bathe you with the cool mist of My Presence. I will hold your hand with tenderness as you lay on your healing bed. I will kiss your heart and make it whole. My divine health and healing is here...in the Vine."

Love the Vinedresser

Chapter 18

The Focus Word

Read 1 Peter 1

I received a short prophetic word that put me on a journey. The word was about "focus".

I hear that "focus" word a lot...."Focus Theresa," says my husband or my son as I tend to get forgetful.

But I sense this word is coming from a loving Father who is beckoning me to draw near, hunker down in the Word, and truly listen to Him.

Here is the word that a dear friend who is a safe place for my heart gave me:

"I just heard that He is revving up your focus. I heard the word keen focus. That you are lifting your head and focusing your face on His eyes. And it's like you see superman, the thing that comes out of His eyes, it's just burning into your eyes. And it's just...I hear that word 'keen' and you are revving up your focus on His face as you are going to need it."

So, one late evening, a night after being given that word, I got out my ipad to read on my Bible App. I was listening to

Holy Spirit, asking Him where He wanted me to set up camp and soak.

I had been in 1 Peter but I felt that nudge to go to 2 Peter Chapter 1.

And then I saw it. Like a lightning bolt, it hit my heart on one verse.

What did I do?

I waited and then spent a long morning asking Holy Spirit to reveal more. So I shared a no bake cookie and drank my coffee with Jesus. (I don't think He took any bites out of the cookie!)

First He told me to read a few other prophetic words in my journal. These are memory stones, gifts, that God gives you. If you don't have any prophetic words given to you, read some of your favorite scripture, or simply go to the Psalms and let God massage your heart.

And then I processed....Or shall I say the Holy Spirit processed me.

How do I have partnership with the divine nature? How do I enhance this idea of living truly in my spirit identity? How do I stay on course to my God given destiny?

I shared this with my Kingdom Mentor/Media Academy members. But I won't leave out this word to you.

Here is the verse:

"And so we have been given the prophetic word...the written message of the prophets, made more reliable and fully validated by the confirming voice of God on the Mount of Transfiguration. **AND YOU WILL CONTINUE TO DO WELL IF YOU STAY FOCUSED ON IT.** For the prophetic message is like a piercing light shining in a gloomy place until the dawning of a new day, when the Morning Star rises in your hearts." 2Peter 1:19 tpt (Bold and caps added for emphasis by me)

Declaration: I am focused on His Word and Spirit in me. I am focusing on His prevailing light in my heart and able to see Him more clearly.

Listen to the Vinedresser

"I am here. Can you see Me? I'm all you need.

"I am here. Now focus on who you are in Me. You don't have to strain or work up something inside you. This is simply who you really are in your spirit identity. Yes, this is the integral part of you, in your spirit, more real than your body. This is where you host My Presence.

"So, drop the drama of the trauma of your mind and focus as you draw close to Me. It's okay child. I know how it hurts or even how you have suppressed the pain. I'm not into digging up the skeletons of the past but excavating My divine power in you, so you can walk above the fray of life in victory.

"Focus on my magnificent promises. Soak your wounds in what I give you in an abundant supply. This piercing focus helps you know Me more intimately.

"Listen. You will never stumble. I have orchestrated and even choreographed the moves for you to make for your healing so fruit will abound. You can find joy even in the crushing. I will enable you to live from barely getting by to flourishing in hope. You can go from striving to abiding, learning the peace of thriving in My Vineyard.

"Here is the fruit you can pick in this garden of My Presence, in knowing intimately my Son Jesus. I'll supplement your spirit identity with goodness, understanding, the strength of self-control, enduring patience, all goodness, godliness, mercy for your brothers and sisters, and finally, an unending love.

"And so my beloved, I'm asking you to align yourself with Me. You will continue to find breakthrough as you stay focused on My Words. I'm all about your destiny, your hopes and dreams.

"Let My promises be a point of convergence to the light of My resplendent love pouring out on you. Let My piercing eyes penetrate and be reflected in yours so you can go into gloomy places carrying My glory and My unending perpetual love for others. I'm all about what matters to you.

"So no strive. Simply abide. In the Vine."
Love the Vinedresser

Chapter 19

Winning Heart Battles

Read Ephesians 6

Pressure. The days you feel worn down amidst pressures compounded.

Battles. The kind of fights that are so intense that internally you feel like you can take no more.

Emotions. Your thoughts and emotions make you feel like you are on a merry-go-round going super fast and it is anything but merry.

I have experienced this in relation to a few issues that are near my heart. I also have a few friends that are in the midst of battles that tear at the seams of their hearts.

One thing I'm learning is to give that pressure back to God by pressing into heaven.

What do I mean by that?

Well, here is one way. The other day I was running errands with Dave determined to not to let the heart issues dominate my emotions, I started to simply praise God and then thank Him for my friend's breakthroughs. I thought of a sister who got a raise and now gets to work from home.

I rejoiced with other ministry friends who received a brand new Lexus as both their cars broke down. I pulled on heaven thanking God for other breakthroughs of reconciliation and restoration going on around me.

Did I feel like doing that amidst my own internal struggles at that moment?

No.

But His voice was so clear to do this. I must say I'm learning so much amidst writing a book about the Breaker Anointing. I laugh to myself thinking I'm getting wrecked to be able to write about this. But one thing is for sure, I'm resolute in obeying what the Holy Spirit says for me to do.

So may I encourage you in this devotional to stay in the Vineyard (Presence) and know you are designed to win these battles. What happens in the external around you does not have to leave you in a pit.

Climb out with praise and thanksgiving...and stand!

Check out Ephesians 6. You may be familiar with the battle gear described here by Paul while he was imprisoned in some dark holes surrounded by big mean guards. He obviously had plenty of time to view these dudes and what they were wearing. Galatians 6 gives us a clue of how God dresses us with armor as we walk with Him. The only parachute

Get a pen and read this Chapter taking notes on what Holy Spirit is saying to you specifically.

I believe firmly that your season is shifting and changing. You have gone through the fire. You have been on the frontline of your own battles. You may still feel the affects of a real spiritual warfare around you.

Hold your ground. Stand. Plant your feet, and your heart, no matter what comes.

Your deliverer is here. I see and declare more answers to your prayers.

I see victory on the other side of the battle.

Make this your declaration:

In The Vine Declaration: I am seated with Christ. I do not let the pressure of the battle stop my destiny. I am a victor!

Listen to the Vinedresser

"Your prayers to Me are more than parachutes with no rip cord jumping out of the plane of your troubling situations.

"I hear you beloved. The battles may rage on around you but I will not leave you defenseless.

"You abide in an intimate position with Me, in the heavenliness. You are seated with Me, remember? Here you live peacefully as My union with you infuses you with My majestic love and favor. You live powerfully as you trust My explosive propensity flowing in and through you. You come from My place of influence and victory. The Vineyard of your heart in Me is greater than the swamp of the world around you.

"Remember beloved, any fight you go thorough is not against flesh and blood but against the principalities and authorities operating in rebellion. They are like the squirm bugs on earth that try to startle you, invading your vineyard (kitchen or living room). Turn the light on...and watch the bug move to a darker place. Spray (speak) to them with your weapon of praying in the Spirit.

"So dear Child, rise up and be strong in the strength of all My might that I give to you. Stand firm in the Vineyard. The schemes of the evil one does not confound or surprise Me as it tries to mess up the garden of your heart. I am the Vinedresser. I have My shotgun to take out the foxes of fear. I will watch over the fruit of your heart.

"Keep talking to Me, My beloved. Bring your prayers before My throne. Your prayers to Me are resounding in heaven as prophetic declarations to direct your family, your state, your nation. I give you My Words to walk, not as a victim but as a victor. Decree and declare what is your inheritance, the divine design of your times.

"You are My conquering warrior. My much loved son. My much loved daughter. It is who you are, in the Vine.

"No strive now child. Simply abide."

Love the Vinedresser

Chapter 20

The Gumby Stretch

Read Philippians 3:12-20

Recently I have had the joy and delightful journey of going through Bethel Atlanta's School of the Supernatural. I feel doubly blessed as my husband Dave gets to share this time with me as we celebrate much loved sons and daughters in our class. I absolutely connect and love our leaders each year.

Just pause with me for a moment on this thought.... Oh how we need our sisters (brothers) in the Lord. They make life so sweet.

Ok ok ok...The VERY FIRST night God had a great Kingdom lesson.

Check this:

One of the leaders had us close our eyes and ask Holy Spirit to picture something He was giving us.

I closed my yes, you know, drawing deep into the well of His Presence. What did I see?

I pictured....GUMBY!

Yes, that little green character that could stretch effortlessly in any direction. (Now if you are the age of my kids, Gumby will not resonate with you).

God says..."Get ready to be flexible and stretch TEE. Some of the stretching will simply be ME extending you to reach more people. Other stretches will involve keeping your joy and peace amidst challenges of balancing a more busy life. I'll always want you to stretch to know Me more and to run hard after My Presence."

After I wrote this thought out on my computer, I look to my left of my journal notes in Evernote and see a word from the Vinedresser...about the stretch! I love Holy Spirit set ups!

So this is the deal friend. The stretch is the test of what and who you will trust. I sense from you that you are really feeling stretched in so many areas...in your finances, your marriage, your relationships, your body, your mind...

Look as the stretch as a good thing. Think of how important it is for your body to stretch before you jog, lift weights, or even walk. You are preparing your body for more!!!

So, God uses the stretch and the test for a good reason. He is laying the foundation for you to handle more and to walk into your destiny with His best plan for you. You are His marathon runner carrying the baton of His Presence to everyone you encounter in the race called life. You are set up already as a winner!

So, Holy Spirit whispered a few of His thoughts on the stretch. Ready first with a declaration?

Declaration: I am being stretched to hold more of His Presence. I enjoy the stretch for more of Him.

Listen to the Vinedresser

"You can handle this stretch my child. I built into your very DNA the ability to hold on with tenacious faith to believe in who you are in the Vine. Just as an Olympic champion continues to train year in and year out, you are My champion designed for a divine purpose to win.

"I will not hold back my tender mercies amidst this grueling process. I will fill you with joy for the journey and unfailing love along the narrow road. Yes, even amidst a rigorous route to My purpose, you can find joy.

"Be confident that nothing you do for Me is a waste of time or effort. Keep your eyes open My Child, and on Me. Hold tight to the Vine. Give it all you got. Be resolute. Love without ceasing. Every stretch makes room for more of My endless love and a deeper intimacy with Me. Train hard. Love always. Extend mercy often.

"The gold I give you will not tarnish like a medal an athlete strives for. You will then realize that the stretch was necessary to actually cross the finish line. Stretch! I am your finish line. Trust Me to bring the victory as you cling to the Vine! "
Love The Vinedresser

Chapter 21

A Salute To The War Horses

Read Song of Songs 8

I get shot at recently.

Well it feels like that every time I shoot a video at this one location at my mother-in-laws house. So here I was sharing in a video basically what is in this chapter and BANG! A very loud and near gunshot went off. This time it did not startle me and it actually fit with what I was saying in the vide. You will have to go to my blog at iKingsMedia.com and look for that video.

Basically in this chapter, I am trying to find the words to explain my heart and how I feel about so many faithful family and friends who have demonstrated the passionate love of God to me through the years.

I thought of my husband. I watch him often how he is so intentional to not walk in the pain or offenses of the past and move on with the love of the Father. He comes alongside friends and leaders and speaks life with prophetic words of hope and healing. His joy overflows with a deep laughter and love stamped on his heart from the Father. He is quick to forgive and slow to anger. He has been radically altered by His Father's love and forever changed.

So I pondered this as I continue to be wrecked by Song of Songs, Chapter 8. I knew there was a word stirring in my heart by the Holy Spirit to let HIM release a Vinedresser Word to you. This word says it all, really.

So, thank you for being a Kingdom War Horse. You truly exemplify one who walks with the breaker anointing. You have travelled through the battle of life pains, being shot at, and wounded. Yet, you allow the Holy Spirit to bring healing to your gaping heart holes and rise as a champion of the faith.

Your life is a safe place for others to rest and process the tangled issues of their life. They find hope in you. They trust you because your life carries the fragrance of His Presence.

I do realize you may not fit this category as you still may have arrows stuck deep in your heart. May I encourage you to forgive. Ask God to bring you someone faithful who will celebrate who you are and not who you are not. Someone who you can throw out an anchor into the stormy seas of your life and they will pull you safely into the harbor of their breakthrough to help you find peace and hope and healing.:

So, this is a tribute to all of you who selfishly toil unseen in the battlefield of life leaving His impression of love and grace:

Declaration: I am a war horse. I am a fierce lover of Jesus able to come to the rescue of those drowning in the sea of religion.

Listen To The Vinedresser:

"Raise your head child. Come inside this garden so you can hear the tender songs of redemption I'm singing over you? My love for you is stronger than the chains of freezing fear that wants to make you feel stuck.

"I have a word of release as you feel like a race horse fastened tight behind the starting gate. My unrelenting and burning fire of My heart is now on your life to shore up your true identity and set you on the road of your desired destiny. I created you like a thoroughbred racehorse, as a forerunner to bringing heaven to earth.

"This is how I experience you. I drink the wine of your devotion as you bring Me perfect happiness, such thrilling joy. You make My heart skip a beat in love for you. Your love for Me enthuses My heart. Do you see My favor pouring out on you as you become a laid down lover? I freely connect you with other followers of My love as you are united in spirit in this Vineyard of My passion and delight.

"This is how I see you. You are now a tower of passion and I call you My beloved. You are a firm wall of peaceful protection for others as you walk in the breaker anointing I have placed on your life. You carry My authority in the spirit realm and are able to speak freedom to my children in harm's way from the evil one. You break asunder the chains on **My** loved one's lives and fear not death, nor the grave.

"This is how I empower you. Your vineyard of love in your heart becomes a feast of hope and help for **My** messengers who have for years been on the battle field serving **Me**. You come alongside these treasured friends of Mine and breathe mercy, grace, and love into their lives. You are a true and tested War Horse with scars to show where you have won life's battles.

"You become their anchor which they can throw into the stormy seas of ministry to simply rest under your compassionate care. They can trust you with their most vulnerable areas of their bruised heart with you because the scent of **My Presence** is all over your life.

"Arise now **My** beloved. Let's dance together in fields of grace and over mountains of fragrant spice. You are my treasured messenger bringing heaven to earth in the promenade of grace, favor, and love, with no striving, simply abiding...in the Vine."

Love the Vinedresser

Chapter 22

Eviction Notice To Fear

Read Zephaniah 3:9-17

I have spent too many years living with the monster of fear. You probably don't need me to spend a lot of time writing about it, although many chapters of this devotional do deal with it.

I know this ugly foul beast has many times made me feel like I was living in a black hole on a deserted island with no family or friends near to rescue m

It has raised up its stupid head in my marriage, my finances, and my parenting.

I hate it. I detest it. So I figure it's time to be fearless and go forward writing to expose its despair while sharing how it can be conquered as I carry the breaker anointing.

It's time for you walk away from it too.

You can do this friend.

Fear wants to keep your mind surrounded in lies about yourself or your situation.

I have written much about a prophetic word the Holy Spirit dropped into my heart one year about Turnaround, stamped with God's grace and favor.

The first part is about the truth this will be the year that your belief systems will align with what God says about you. You get that through declarations which spring from the Word of God.

The second part flows from this first component of declarations. This simply means it time to put an eviction notice to your fears.

I had Zephaniah 3:9-14 in the Message as the basis for this word. Look at verses 15-17.

"From now on, God is Israel's king,
in charge at the center.
There's nothing to fear from evil
ever again!
God Is Present Among You
Jerusalem will be told:
"Don't be afraid.
Dear Zion,
don't despair.
Your God is present among you,
a strong Warrior there to save you.
Happy to have you back, he'll calm you with his love
and delight you with his songs."

Zephaniah 3:14-17 MSG

I truly believe as you learn to enter His Presence (no strive) and walk in faith of His love, fear will have to go. In His Presence is fullness of joy (Psalm 16:11), not fear.

Since I'm still a work in progress with this issue, I asked Holy Spirit for a simple declaration and a word from the Vinedresser.

Declaration: I will not walk in fear but in love. My Warrior-Jesus-is near.

Listen to the Vinedresser

"Dear child. That monster of fear that has been chasing you for so long is defeated. When your heart feels like its raging with trepidation, draw nearer and deeper into My garden.

"Let me calm you. Let me love You where panic has ravaged your heart and where your emotions have been on a merry-go-round going way too fast. Soak in the peaceful pool of My tender love. My Spirit is gentle to cleanse your wounds from trauma that tries to take up residence in your heart.

"Come now into this Vineyard and experience My Presence. Here you can feel the gentle beats of My heart as I hold you close. My love is stronger than these chains of horror. I am the fire and light inside of you. I will never leave you in the dark or out in the cold. Fear with its fruit of pain and persecution will never quench the raging fire of love I lit inside of you.

"I am near. My love will capture you and you will never be the same. Watch how I can bring back what the enemy has stolen. Join the parade of My lovers rejoicing and dancing in the streets of freedom. Do you hear that? It's time for you to rejoice My love. You can join the chorus and sing 'My Father is the King of My heart...My Father loves me....He is a good Father...'

"Yield to My furious and unrelenting love. Your faith in My majestic love makes you hell's furry. The enemy has no power over you. You are not a friend of fear. You are a friend of Me. Your breakthroughs of squashing your agitation of worry makes you a carrier of My Presence, helping others to do the same around you. Remember now... No performance needed child. No strive but abide....in the Vine."

Love the Vinedress

Chapter 23

Embrace The Yuck

Read 2 Peter 1

After a July 4th weekend of one sweet moment after another with lifer friends, I hit my emotional toe on a "sucky" misfire in communication.

So I had to shift my mindset and "embrace the suck." (Pardon me if that is offensive to you)

What does this mean?

It is a military term. What it means is "when we deny what reality is giving us, what is really happening, then we create suffering. So life is a dance between minimizing expectations and surrendering to what our lives actually reveal to us."

I asked Holy Spirit on this and He said...Surrender EVERYTHING TO ME. This is those times when you learn to praise and trust Me right where you are...and set your mind on what I SAY."

He said...

"Grace and peace be multiplied to you in the knowledge of God and of Jesus our Lord, as His divine power has given to us all things that pertain to life and godliness, through the knowledge of Him who called us by glory and virtue, by which have been given to us exceedingly great and precious promises, that through these you may be partakers of the divine nature, having escaped the corruption that is in the world through lust." 2 Peter 1:2-4 **NKJV** (Read on for the next verses for more truth of this!)

So to embrace anything that seems to hurt you, something that does not go your way, a feeling of insecurity, or even a stall in your destiny, God has given you a gift of walking in the power of your divine nature in your mind. You can control **HOW** your react.

When you see the situation from the perspective of the way God sees you, and the trouble, you are loaded with promises from the Word to prevail. You are also empowered to walk in your true identity being spirit lead, partakers of His divine nature in you as you go through life embracing **HIS** Word and empowering His declarations over your life.

And... you are given the power of choice. The choice to not let the situation rule your life. The choice to cry out to Him for help. The choice to forgive and ask for forgiveness. The choice to praise Him in the storm.....The choice to ask a few close friends to help you by speaking life over you... The choice to take a step in faith and believe He will always help you through the circumstance. The choice to sing allowing His joy be your strength.

These choices have the power to change you, transform your mind, and help you walk in your true identity as a spirit lead Kingdom shaker for heaven.

God sees you as wonderful, powerful, and able to persevere. He calls you His much loved son. His much loved daughter.

Corrie ten Boom used to say,

"When the train goes through a tunnel and the world gets dark, do you jump out? Of course not. You sit still and trust the engineer to get you through."

Did you know He is just a breath away? His arms are open to take the misery (yuck) and reveal your destiny. He embraces you always.

Declaration: I can take my present chaotic emotions and circumstance and leave them with Jesus. I am being embraced by His grace, not the yuck.

Listen To The Vinedresser

"I am only a breath away. Speak My name often and come into My Vineyard. Here you experience the unforced rhythms of My heart beat as I breath My deep peace and never ending love over you. Not even the recent chaotic emotions of the process can close the doors from experiencing more of Me.

"As you enter this quiet place I take you into My arms. Instantly the smell of fear vanishes and is replaced by the fragrance from the healing oil of My Spirit. I take such great pleasure in you My Child. I feel immense joy that you have ran across the mine fields of your circumstances to be wrapped in the Secret Place in my garden.

"You are mine beloved. And all of Me is yours. Taste and see that I am good. Open your eyes to the radiant glory of My Spirit rising in you. Let the issues go. In my Love, there is always a reward to the seeker and the one who is quick to forgive.

"My promises are yes and amen. I heard your yes as you have diligently changed your direction to come back to Me here to rest. Allow the sun to shine on your face. Feel the warmth of My embrace.

"Enter often. You are on My assignment watch. In you is your purpose to shine with radiance shifting and influencing every place you enter. You bring the anointing. It's in you.

"These are not terror days. These are days of stories of glory. And He is going to heal you, use you, save your family, raise the dead, cast out the evil...bringing heaven to earth.

"It's all in the abiding dear one. Not in striving. In the Vine."

Love The Vinedresser

Chapter 24

Open Door

Mathew 13:1-23

I see an open door for you with the turnaround that is coming. Yes, the turnaround stamped with all of God's favor and grace. No matter the trials you may feel open doors are here.

Even though, I have literally hit a wall with struggles from a wreck, and watching my husband experience gut wrenching pain, one truth remains. As I quote Dave:

"No circumstance or hardship, nor crisis, or lack of physical healing, could ever cause a limitation on the Holy Spirit's ability to flow out of you." Firebrand Dave

He is a miracle working God fulfilling His promises, even behind the scenes. He is moving in and through you.

So, keep trusting and walking. It might be a fight at times to just keep it together. But your are not too far gone. Hope is never lost. The shift in the turnaround is this fact:

God is establishing His remnant into position to not falter, even when the doctor, or the teacher, or the specialists news is bad.

You are going to be ok.

I believe He has open doors to the supernatural realm for you now to mirror what's in heaven. You take that reflection and shine it on your circumstances. And then watch! You become a magnet for all of God's goodness, grace, and mercy for more!

You stride into the breaker anointing with His DNA moving in you to impact more hearts with the hope of heaven. Reach and walk through this open door by faith and belief.

I believe God holds the light at the end of the tunnel and the answers to your prayers. I see turnaround for you with all of God's grace and favor behind it!

Listen! The Vinedresser is speaking to you with this declaration:

Declaration: I will walk through God's open doors. What God opens no one will shut. What door God shuts, no one will open. I believe in my miracle working God.

Listen To The Vinedresser

"There is a shifting. Re-alignment is coming. With this comes a new door to open for you My beloved. The password is praise and a yes from your heart.

"Watch My yes collide with yours and see an outpouring of all my good and precious promises. This will be a time where you see it's been worth the wait as your turnaround begins.

"So, don't fret child. I see how you get down and how tired the pressing issues are on your heart. Lift up your head. My faithfulness is here. You can trust Me....

"Do you see the open door before you? It's Me leading the way. You cried out and I came to you. Now, come in and let's dine together on the feast I have created in this intimate spot. You can get your fill of the grapes with their miracle working nourishment.

"My Presence is constant and flowing with My wine of revelation. Add your laid down heart of praise and worship and experience a most sweet fragrance that instantly refreshes your soul.

"Your messes don't move me. Your unresolved issues in your family are not road blocks. Your prayers for your wandering child or family member are always heard. Your physical pain does not mean I don't heal. Hold on. Don't let go. I am a miracle working God.

"Listen and be attentive as you take this step through love's open door. Keep saying yes in this secret place of My heart, I bring forth a never ending flow of My goodness and My favor into your life.

"This brings the peace you crave, the hope you long for, the healing that makes everything ok. So take courage my Child. All this and more simply flows from your identity as you come to understand I am always good; I call you My child; My love is here to amaze you and wrap around your heart. My kindness will astound you as you see Me fulfill My promises in your life.

"So take My hand and lets go through this new door I open. No strive. Just abide."

Love the Vinedresser

Chapter 25

Held In The Grip Of Grace

Read Romans 4 and 5

I had these Christmas thoughts a while back. Simply this:

Held in the grip of grace... That's where I long to be.

As the sounds of the movie Elf echo in the background with grandkids giggles, I ponder Chapter 4 and 5 in Romans.

This verse captures my heart...

"Death once held us in its grip, and by the blunder of one man, death reigned as king over humanity. But now, how much more are we held in the grip of grace and continue reigning as kings in life, enjoying our regal freedom through the gift of perfect righteousness in the one and only Jesus, the Messiah!" Romans 5:17 TPT

Held in the grip of grace. Reigning as kings in life. Enjoying freedom. The gift of righteousness alive in me. The one and only Jesus.

What does this mean to you?

May I suggest....

No matter how issues and fears want to try and strangle you by the neck, they can't. You are held by His grace. There is nothing you have to do but simply REST and abide in this grace, as you embrace HIM as your first love.

No matter how lack wants to tackle you and slam you down, it can't. You are called to reign in life.

No matter how disconnected you may feel with family or friends, you are always connected to the One who restores and replenishes.

Capping these truths is the fact that He, who knew no sin, became sin on your behalf so you may be called the righteousness of God. (See 2 Corinthians 5:21)

"It's a gift. Perfect righteousness with a relationship more close than any friendship with Jesus. (God fully reconciled us to himself through the death of his Son, then something greater than friendship is ours." Romans 5:10 TPT

Amazing gifts from a Father who adores and loves you.

Simple thoughts a day after Christmas.

And a simple word Declaration and word from your Vinedresser.

Declaration: I thank God for the "present" He give me in each new day. I am held in His grip of grace.

Listen To The Vinedresser

"Dear child. I love you. I will continue to give you each day with more presents containing My Presence. Don't fret. I won't drop your heart's desires or destiny dreams. I hold you close to My Heart, in the grip of grace.

"I see you as flawless in My eyes. You have access to My marvelous kindness and radiant love. My Heart burst with joy every time you draw near to me. You make my heart skip a beat.

"Don't think I have forgotten your heart's plea for restoration in your family, your finances, even your faith. I have all the pieces and will put them beautifully together leaving you a legacy that has extended from your intimacy with you.

"Even as you experience troubles and pressures, know that I am working in you patient endurance. Your character will be refined like gold. Hope will be restored as you continue to experience my never ending love that washes over you through the Holy Spirit.

"I am not into disappointing fantasy. I am all about your destiny. I am into you. You are into Me. And we will dance for all eternity.

"Merry Christmas and love...The Vinedresser"

Chapter 26

Communion: A Word From The Son

Read Mathew 26:17-30

During communion today the thought of rest came to my heart.

Communion: Taking some grape juice and a cracker and "doing this in remembrance" of Him.

This is the thought that came with it.

We can get caught up in the "do do do" of life that we simply forget to rest, and listen to God.

This is not just a spiritual rest but also for our souls.

The more I study and learn about soul health the more I realize how important unity in your spirit is to your soul.. This unity involves the confession of sin. Yes, the sin of ours and others which causes soul wounds, and brings the trauma and drama to emotions.

This has to come to a place of release.

When we allow our wounds to fester through un-forgiveness and offense, it affects our very body.

Our souls, traumatized by sin and the affect of internal injury, make our bodies fertile ground for sickness, disease, and addictions.

Which brings me to communion.

The last supper Jesus had before His crucifixion was during the Passover feast, or known as The Feast Of Unleavened Bread. This represented the time going back to the days when the Israelites put blood on their door posts so God would passover and not kill their first born.

And now, during this feast of remembrance, here sits God's first born, Jesus, having this last supper with His disciples, His friends.

"As they were eating, Jesus took some bread and blessed it. Then he broke it in pieces and gave it to the disciples, saying, "Take this and eat it, for this is my body."

"And he took a cup of wine and gave thanks to God for it. He gave it to them and said, "Each of you drink from it, for this is my blood, which confirms the covenant[b] between God and his people. It is poured out as a sacrifice to forgive the sins of many. Mark my words—I will not drink wine again until the day I drink it new with you in my Father's Kingdom." Matthew 26:26-29 NKJV

"When Jesus became our sacrifice, he made the way for our prayers, praises, and worship to become like that incense to the Lord...." Kelly Willard

Hence, I have been compelled to ask my Kingdom Mentor/Media Academy group to join me in daily communion for at least a week. We had our first communion LIVE on video in the group this recently. It was a community event of love and honor, together, for our Savior Jesus.

I know the Vinedresser has a word on this. Well, actually the Son of the Vinedresser. My friend, Jesus, was speaking gently in my heart with this simple declaration:

Declaration: I am thankful for You sacrifice Jesus so I can have abundant life now. I am Your delight.

Listen To the Son of the Vinedresser:

"Dear friend of Mine. I see the travail of your soul resulting in disorder in your mind and emotions. This internal agony is affecting your body, dear friend. That pain. That sickness. That heart wrenching rattle bringing darkness to your soul.....

"Come to Me. Rest. The anguish of your soul can soak in the kindness of grace I lavish on you. The agony from the recesses of your heart is spilling out causing an upheaval around you. Your "do do do" list is leaving you spent and broken.

"Hey, listen. This is The Vine, Jesus, talking to you friend. Do you remember?

"I drank the cup of suffering for you. I was afflicted and tormented on the cross. The work is finished. My body was broken bread and poured out wine just for you.

"And now, I am no longer in the tomb. You could be healed of all your wounds. The resurrection power is at work in you.

"Let's do this together friend, in remembrance. Break the cracker or tear off a piece of bread.

"Pour the wine. I hear your cry asking for forgiveness and I rejoice with your heart as you bring your tender thanksgivings to Me.

"Take. Eat. Drink. Do this now in remembrance of Me.

"I am your song that never stops reaching for you in the deep abyss of your heart.

"You have stolen My heart.

"I am your lover and friend who is relentless in keeping you close.

"I am undone by your love.

"I am your Shepherd watching like a hawk over you and your family.

"I am held hostage by your love.

"I am your true and faithful healer of your soul.

"Your love is my finest wine.

"I am who I am.

"Your praise is My priceless perfume.

"I am the Son of the Vinedresser. I am the Vine. And you are Mine."

Love the Son of the Vinedresser

Chapter 27

Validation: The More Than Enough Anointing

Read Exodus 36

Can validation bring the more than enough anointing?

I say yes and find one of many answers in the Word.

The part of the definition of validation is this: "recognition or affirmation that a person or their feeling or opinions are valid and worthwhile."

I've seen this validation have a powerful effect on a person's growth from my family to my friends.

What if it is lacking? Well for one, it's easy to be offended and lose your identity if you are constantly looking for it from others.

So, how does validation bring the more than enough anointing?

Well, let's make one thing very clear. The only true place for real validation can be found in your intimacy with Jesus, in the Secret Place of His Presence.

Write that down. Validation comes from knowing who you are in Christ! (Your spirit identity).

I love this story in Exodus 36 when the Israelites were building the Temple. I encourage you to go and read that passage.

Here you see Moses (Starting in Exodus 35:30) explaining how two men were gifted by the Lord as skilled craftsmen who were summoned to lead the building of the Temple.

Talk about validation!

But I love the eagerness of those who may not have been mentioned by name—they knew their value and did not need Moses affirmation—and they were eager to work!

"So Moses summoned Bezalel and Oholiab and all the others who were specially gifted by the Lord and were eager to get to work." Exodus 36:2 NLT

As you go on in this chapter in Exodus, you see the people giving and giving...and the "more than enough" that followed. The craftsmen went to Moses to tell him...

"They went to Moses and reported, "The people have given more than enough materials to complete the job the Lord has commanded us to do!" Exodus 36:5 NLT

I believe this Word is for you. Look for the Lord to bring you His affirmation and your identity in Him.

And watch the more than enough anointing spill out of your life into not just your finances, but your healing, reconciliation, and soul health.

Here's a declaration and a word from the Vinedresser just for you

Declaration: I know who I am in Christ. I am His much loved daughter, His much loved son. I have more than enough.

Listen to the Vinedresser..

"I am walking amidst you saying I am all you need. I am more than enough no matter what you are facing. Your sweet devotion and tender worship here in this place, is a sweet aroma... Do you hear me?.... I am all you need. I am more than enough. I declare a more than enough declaration over this land, over your family, over your life.

"I am giving you an intimate experience of deep insight into the hidden truths and mysteries of my realm here in this garden. It is the realm of My Kingdom which you have access anytime of any day. Here is the storehouse for wealth in revelation that is more than enough for you.

"As I hear you sing that you want more of Me, I am releasing my breaker anointing that pours the more than enough fire. The fire breaks open the ground of your heart so you cant be able to handle well the overpowering depth of my Majestic love and grace... The fire burns off the imperfections. Don't worry, My Child, My oil is here to soothe any pain of the flame on your skin.

"Watch the release of MORE of Me...I am declaring that this land will be a land of reconciliation. From the east to the west...from nation to nation... More of My Presence will flow. You will be My Hands, My feet, My mouth...You will know how and when to bring the treasures in your heart to show to others.

"So go ahead. Ask for more. Ask for more! I delight to give to my laid down lovers the anointing of more. Finances? Consider it done. Relationships? Consider them restored.. Bodies wracked with pain? Consider them healed.

"The more than enough is here... For what I have stored up in your hearts will be heard by your generation with the overflow of your words. You will be My forerunners of the more than enough messengers. Remember, the more than enough hidden truth comes not by striving, but simply abiding, in the Vine.

Love The Vinedresser

Chapter 28

Keys Of Favor

Read Psalm 75:6-7

I am praying for God's favor on your life. And I believe He's handing out keys to open doors of favor for you...now!

I say this with the utmost confidence that He has designed it for you. I did a simple word search in Scriptures on favor and like a tidal wave God's promises hit me.

His promises? Yes and AMEN in Christ Jesus.

"For all the promises of God in Him are Yes, and in Him Amen, to the glory of God through us." 2 Corinthians 1:20 NKJ

And let's be clear on a simple truth. God is the ONLY one who can grant favor before Himself and with men:

"This I know: the favor that brings promotion and power doesn't come from anywhere on earth, for no one exalts a person but God, the true judge of all. He alone determines where favor rests. He anoints one for greatness and brings another down to his knees."

Psalm 75:6-7 tpt

This can keep you from striving to please everyone. As you do you work as unto God, you can be confident no matter how tough your boss or situation is, God still is the one who can give you favor.

And I truly believe He's handing out these keys for favor right now!

I was asking Holy Spirit for three key chain holders to give you a chance to formulate your own focus word on favor. He gave me the acronym G-O-D. Easy to remember.

So...get a pen and paper out to write the meaning of each layer.

G- Gratefulness. God so loves a grateful heart no matter what is going on. Gratefulness is the door to favor.

"You can pass through his open gates with the password of praise.
Come right into his presence with thanksgiving.
Come bring your thank offering to him
and affectionately bless his beautiful name!" Psalm 100:4 tpt

O-Obedience. To love Him is to obey Him. As you love Him you realize quickly you don't want to hurt His Heart. This is the key that opens the door and it's the ultimate form of worship. I love this verse...reminding me that not only favor but HIS AFFECTION is toward me as I obey Him.

D-Discipleship: Discipleship is the reality of living with the favor of God in your life. This is simply walking as a revivalist. You cultivate and keep intimate devotion to Jesus. You walk in your spirit identity in authority. You bring revival because revival lives in you. You continue to grow in Him with the Word of God as light to your path.

"The child grew more powerful in grace, for he was being filled with wisdom, and the favor of God was upon him." Luke 2:40 tpt

God is positioning you in sphere of influence where you can handle the favor.

Look for it...in your family, in your workplace, in your finances. It's not just about you but those God has called you to impact. His FAVOR will help you talk to your flock.

I shared more on this topic with specific declarations and prayers over the family in my Kingdom Mentor/Media Academy.

Let's get to this declaration and word from the Vinedresser

Declaration: I have the favor of God in my life. It is a reality of being in the Vine with gratefulness, obedience, and growth as His revivalist.

Listen to the Vinedresser:

"My favor wraps around you and covers you with my affection, kindness and joy. Favor goes before you for increase in every area of your life. I long to be extravagant and generous every time you hide yourself in Me, in the Vine. So dear child, remain grateful as you rest in My soil of goodness and mercy.

"In this Vineyard you will find the secret of growing in the delight and favor of My ways. Favor brought my daughter Esther before a King. It will do the same for you as I extend open doors and pleasures of spiritual wealth. I place My breaker anointing on you to to blast through brick walls with My dripping oil of tender love and amazing grace on those around you.

"Look intently as I champion your heart's desire making you a mighty warrior filled to overflowing with the treasure of My affection. I am here to give you strength, wise strategy, and revelation insight to take your mountain of influence, in your family, in the arts, in the marketplace, in education, in government, in ministry.

"Did I tell you? I love your grateful heart. I see your obedience, even when no one is looking. You are my revivalist changing the atmosphere for my glory everywhere you walk. You are the revival people are looking for because I put revival in your heart.

"So my dear beloved, I extend My favor to you every time you approach Me with humility. You can be sure I will back you in every endeavor. In My favor is My anointing for you to bring others into My vineyard of love and grace. Abide in this favor today.

No strive My beloved. Simply abide."

Love the Vinedresser

Chapter 29

Spark To Destiny Delay

Read Psalm 25

Do you feel like destiny delay has hit you? I remember feelings like this in regards to my dreams or even what I had imagined.

I remember the feelings. It was as if I was left on the back burner with the heat still on. It's hot, dry, and it even hurts back there.

Or can you relate to this? Maybe a financial crash has hit you hard. You lost your job. You got in an accident. Your child got sick.

Zap. There goes another wall in front of going forward.

Are there really steps to walk out your destiny and your dreams?

YES!

I shared four steps last week with our Kingdom Mentor/Media Academy Group.

One step I shared was to go back in your memory and remember: What did you pretend or dream of doing and you played that out as a child? What did you enjoy doing as a child.?

Did you play house...did you play with dolls...did you construct things?

I know I was big into sports with four brothers. I loved all sports but eventually excelled in the game of golf. I won many local tournaments and eventually traveled as a junior golfer and later in the collegiate field. I was All-American my junior year and eventually turned pro touring the country.

As strong as my desire was to make it in professional golf, my dreams came crashing down. I remember one thing I imagined: If I can't make it to the LPGA league, I'd like to work at a Christian Radio Station as an announcer.

Well, that imagination dream became reality as I retired from golf. I miraculously got a job as an announcer in a very competitive and rare job opening field. I eventually spent the next 15 1/2 years at a major FM Christian radio station outside of Atlanta as an announcer.

All of this reflection reminded me of my imagination as a six to eight year old. I would sneak and get my dad's (modern technology for that day) tape recorder and talk and talk for hours into that little mic. I loved microphones by the way. I loved to imagine I was Walter Cronkite or Carol Burnett.

I also loved to pretend to be a preacher. (Never mind I grew up Catholic). I'd tip over apple carts and preach to my little brother. When he got bored, I'd tell the rocks and flowers they needed to repent and be saved.

Anyway...I think you get the idea.

But I do understand that over time negative junk comes to your mind and toxicity gets in to your brain where all you see is the lies the enemy wants you to believe.

But as you go through a process and really learn more about your new identity and walk it out, your brain can recalibrate!

It's a process.

As I was teaching my Kingdom mentor group, I had this thought of...

"A Cigarette lighter"!

Think of the friction it takes with your thumb to get a flame out of that cig lighter. (We can call it destiny lighter.) That is the friction, the tension, the stress, the drama, the action to get something started. You have to move that thumb and trust what's inside to make a flame to the spark.

And get this, the fluid inside the lighter is the Holy Spirit!

So, listen. IF your thumb (or whatever) is sore and tired. Take heart. You have the real thing inside you...the Holy Spirit. Have you ever thought that the friction to your destiny might be in the spiritual realm where the enemy knows the ground you will take from him as you succeed in what your are called to do.

Destiny friction and resistance. I think it's evidence you are on the right track!

I believe in you. I believe God put in you a destiny where others are going to be impacted mightily. You are an amazing mom. You are a skilled and favor marketplace man. You are a world changer. You have an extra ordinary solution to someone's pain point.

Go through the process friend. Create some sparks. Get over your hurting thumb and believe.

I believe in you. I value you too. So dream on and use your imagination!!

Declaration: I can imagine with God attaching His faith to my visions. What I did as a child can be a blueprint for my destiny.

Listen to the Vinedresser

"I gave you your mind child to soar in your imagination like an eagle. Your imagination is a gift so you can activate dreams that I have designed for you to fulfill. My Eyes twinkled with delight as I saw you dance and dream as a child, acting on the very destiny plan I place in you for dreams coming true.

"Fill your thoughts and meditate on all that is authentic and real, compelling and gracious--the best not the worst. You can imagine with Me as you desire to be whole, emotionally and physically. Walk in your spirit identity and be lead by the value of peace in your heart.

"Look at Me and see your future! Reject striving. You don't have to make it happen. Rest in the power of the supernatural I placed in you child. Believe you carry the DNA to accomplish what I designed in you since birth. Just as a earthly father celebrates the steps of a baby, so I celebrate your progress.

"Forget looking at your past and letting it define your future. Your destiny in Me is not based on failure but on who I say you are and who you are becoming in the Vine! So, use your imagination to activate My purposes in you to create, empower, inspire and visualize My promises fulfilled in you!

So no strive. Simply abide in the Vine."

Love the Vinedresser

Chapter 30

Keys And Open Doors

Mathew 13:1-23

God recently said to me.... "Speak more prophetic words here in book form and on social media."

Challenging, but yet becoming easier as I surrender to Him.

I believe you can speak and grow in a gift called the prophetic too.

Can I explain and then share a recent word?

So here is one verse from The Passion Translation that helps explain to me how this can be.

"He explained, 'You've been given the intimate experience of insight into the hidden truths and mysteries of the realm of heaven's kingdom, but they have not. For everyone who listens with an open heart will receive progressively more revelation until he has more than enough. Matt 13:11-12 TPT

So my prayer is to learn the mysteries of the Kingdom, to ask for spirit revelation...straight from God. I don't want to be in a striving mode with this either. So I ask like a child to my Father...open my eyes dear Lord.

One other key I found the other morning in John 17:10:

"For all who belong to me
Now belong to you.
And all who belong to you
Now belong to me as well,
And my glory is revealed
Through their surrendered lives."
John 17:10 tpt

So God's glory is not revealed in my striving, nor performance. No matter how great I speak or write for Him, this is not what shines.

It is in my surrender to Him...Being a laid down lover of Jesus.

From this place of rest, I can live and walk in the design of the very DNA He stamped in my life. So from the everyday chore of doing laundry, to shooting a video, or simply being by my husband's side speaking life over His messengers, God's glory can be revealed by simply who I am in the vine.

"For what has been stored up in your hearts will be heard in the overflow of your words!" Matt 12:34 TPT

One morning in church in Jacksonville, Florida the Vinedresser spoke a prophetic word to me. It was a little bit different.

As the word came He reminded me that you can release the tune of heaven which produces a domino affect of changed lives and more new songs resounding with sweet and tender sounds from high places in heaven!

He is giving you the keys. The song will come as you unlock the doors in front of you.

Use it on yourself. Unlock your heart and sing! Someone is waiting for you!

It was quite exciting later in the day as we were walking the streets of downtown Jacksonville to see a giant key and lock catty corner to the building of a huge old closed church where our friend's have a vision for to be messengers of hope to that area.

It's okay to ask how the door will open and where the sound will come.

Simply remember, in the process of abiding comes the opening of doors......in your heart and in your life.

So...here is an "overflow" that came to me as I sat in church. I believe this word and declaration might be just for you"

Declaration: God has open doors for me to walk through. I will bring HIS sound to every place I walk.

Listen to the Vinedresser:

"I am here beloved handing out keys, lots of keys into hands of My much loved sons and daughters. The keys unlock the doors of the high and low places of life. I will direct you to each door of influence.

"As you unlock the doors you are bringing a new song, My sound, from the very heart of heaven, with a cadence rich in beauty and majesty. These songs break chains and open new doors for people bound by addictions, ensnared by greed, and fenced in by offense.

"Open your hand dear Child. The keys I'm giving you also get you in doors of government, with high ranking officials, and wealthy men and woman. I have spoken to them in dreams and visions. Some know Me. Some do not but are looking for the real ME as I've put a spiritual hunger in their very soul.

"You get to use these keys and every door unlocked you enter bringing the Father's heart. Turn the key in faith. Speak boldly yet tenderly to these men and women dominating their sphere of influence.

"You, My dear child, release the tune which produces a domino affect of changed lives and more new songs resounding with sweet and tender sounds from high places in heaven!

"Yes, I am giving you the keys. The song will come as you unlock the doors in front of you.

"Use it on yourself. Unlock your heart and sing! Someone is waiting for you! Someone is waiting to listen and drink the wine of your devotion to Me.

"I love you. I am proud of you. You have great value."

Love the Vinedresser

Chapter 31

Sweet Marriage In The Vine

Mathew 13:1-23

I'm really struggling with this last chapter

It's like I'm squirming with my back against the wall.

But I heard the Holy Spirit say to write about this....marriage, sweet marriage, in the vine.

At first I passed it off with a thought.. "I may be married for over 21 years but I am not the expert on this one.."

Or...

"Come on! Taking the mask off will feel like ripping open a sealed wound. Really God?"

The thought persisted. I really do not want to disobey what He tells me to do even if I feel my failures are so many and my story so broken. But I'm learning that pleasing God and obeying Him is yet one of many ways I get to love Him back.

This thought on writing about my marriage did make me think about how in the past few years God has allowed us to be broken bread and spilled out wine for others to find nourishment, to make their marriages work.

One after another broken winged bird has come to our nest (home), where Dave and I have been able to reveal our marriage failures and success to help others get breakthrough in their own relationships. I also realize my mom and father left a legacy of this as I recalled the few couples they ministered to who were on the brink of separation. My parents were not shaken and stuck with these dear friends speaking life, and their marriages were restored.

So, I step out here to share with you in this devotional. I know this is one thing He has called me to do. It comes with the breaker anointing He placed on my marriage and my family. You break off the weights of failure to be able to lift others, by speaking Kingdom life and sharing the Father's heart. My breakthrough is your breakthrough friend!

One thing is for sure....We each have our own story to tell. I will simply share mine with hopes you can get off the emotional ledge and find a more secure place to stand, in hope, faith, and love.

Let me hit the low points where I have been found in many years of being married.

The major factor? I was living in the trenches of my own making. The battle was in one word: FEAR!

This kept me locked in a prison with the keys to be free but I didn't use them.

I was a walking facade. Walking in deception of who I was and who God made me to be. I was afraid I'd be found out and ridiculed.

I could readily put up an appearance of normal, but abnormal was stuck on the inside as anxiety sucked away my stamina and strength.

I dealt with oppression that became depression.

Even though my husband was an amazingly skilled in everything from construction to drywall to landscaping, I faced a debt monster that could never be satisfied.

Confrontation sent me to a deserted island to take part in a beach pity party with me drinking the alcohol of irresponsibility and the sour grapes of anguish.

My goal became disconnect and avoidance which lead to judgement.

Dysfunction became a sick normal, stuck like a piece of gum on the bottom of your shoe.

This final reality broke my heart and made me realize I had to ask God to help me.

My husband and my two children did not really know me.

Thud.

Now, I will tell you that amidst this mess I did find hope and help. It was in my coveted time alone with a cup of coffee, the Word, my jagged heart, and my journal. Out of the overflow I was able to speak and pray hope over thousands.

Of all places, God put me behind a mic on a Christian FM radio station that all of Atlanta and North Georgia could hear for over 15 years. Part of the time I was single while the other married.

As I tried to be free from fear choking at my jugular vein, I wrote out my issues with the Word of God as the back drop in dozens of journals. So often the word would bring healing and hope as I asked God to change me.

I began to understand boundaries. I stopped making excuses empowering the well planned lies. I began to call those things that were not to be manifested. To be honest, this scared the heck out of me. I began to pray....getting in to my own "war room", decreeing and declaring the truth of what God says. I began to pray in the Holy Spirit like my life depended on it.

I will tell you this. I never empowered the lie that I made a mistake. I look at my children and see no mistake there. Even before I had children, I knew that I knew, that God put Dave and me together to bring change and impact others for the Kingdom of God.

So if you can relate to any of the facts of my struggle above, let me assure you God will not leave you. He will honor your effort and give grace for every step. (I will say if you are in severe physical or emotional abuse, you need to seek wise counsel or simply get away to a safe place.)

Today, I feel like I have stepped out of a shadow of fear and face my struggles head on with His Spirit. Dave and I are going on our 22nd year of marriage. He is truly my best friend.

I thank God for the new moments of knowing this handsome, God fearing, Kingdom shaking man who God brought to me. His tenderness and care reveals so many facets of the Father's Heart to me daily. He inspires me and empowers me with daily prayers and declarations. He celebrates me in my dream to be a voice, a mentor, to be a life speaker, to be an author of influence for the Kingdom of God.

This probably won't be the end of writing about this tender subject of relationships and marriage. But I pray my taking the mask off and revealing my failures will help you see your are not alone.

I understand the pain and frustration. Focus on you. Keep your boundaries in tack. And always, be found often in the Vineyard, in the Vine, listening to the Vinedresser of your heart, mind, spirit, and soul.

For this final chapter, you will still hear from the Vinedresser. But He will be speaking as the lover of your soul.

Declaration: I am loved. He is able to take that which is broken and make it whole. He is the lover of my soul. I am His bride.

Listen to the The Lover of Your Soul

"My love and grace has a face. Come closer dear child. Look Me in My eyes. Listen as I speak to you as My beloved. Do you know how I long for an intimate union with you, a divine romance that starts with a kiss, a face to face encounter?

"I am all about relationship where My love is a rushing river to wash your sin and make you ever beautiful in My sight. I am not into scaring you but loving you into this intimate friendship. My caresses are kind. My Presence brings an aroma from My Vineyard, sweet smells of growing fruit. I long to dine with you drinking the sweet wine of your devotion with uninhibited bliss and joy.

"Your anguish from your wrecked relationships do not move me or repel me. Let Me apply the oil of My Presence and the Blood of My Son to those ravished wounds, as I heal your mind from the drama of the trauma."

"I adore you beloved. I value you. Your love for Me makes my heart skip a beat. Let's dance together. Let me twirl you with My tender love leading you with steps toward healing and hope.

"I am your Bridegroom King. You are My bride."

Love The Lover of Your Soul

About

Theresa Croft, 'the media messenger', is a wife, mom and a Kingdom revivalist/media influencer. She is creator of the #inthevine and "Listen To The Vinedresser" Movement online.

Theresa helps leaders discover their true identity so they have the resources and capacity to succeed in their calling. She is like a coach sending in strategic calls to you, the quarterback, so you can score more destiny touchdowns in life.

Theresa teaches in her Kingdom Mentor/Media Academy. She is also a Social Media Consultant, Video Producer and Life Speaker.

She is also the author of two other books: "Volume 1 - Listen To The Vinedresser: 31 Declarations Of Who You Are In The Vine" and "The Spirit Identity Series: Four Steps To Walking Spirit Driven"

For speaking engagement, contact her at TheMediaMessenger@gmail.com

Follow the Theresa On The Web:

iKingsMedia.com
Facebook.com/TheresaMCroft
YouTube.com/c/theresacroft
Instagram.com/theresacroft

Made in the USA
Coppell, TX
30 December 2022